T. Fisher

**A yachting cruise to Norway**

T. Fisher

**A yachting cruise to Norway**

ISBN/EAN: 9783743316317

Manufactured in Europe, USA, Canada, Australia, Japa

Cover: Foto ©Andreas Hilbeck / pixelio.de

Manufactured and distributed by brebook publishing software (www.brebook.com)

T. Fisher

**A yachting cruise to Norway**

# A YACHTING CRUISE
# TO NORWAY

BY

THE PARSON AND THE LAWYER

London:
T. FISHER UNWIN
PATERNOSTER SQUARE

MDCCCXCV

# CONTENTS

### CHAPTER I.

Choosing a Holiday—Norway—Inland Tour or Yachting Cruise—Conflicting Opinions, . . . . . PAGE 1

### CHAPTER II.

Bank Holiday Travelling—Lost Luggage—The *Venus*—Sailing from the Tyne — Feeding Arrangements on Board—Our Table, . . . . . . . 10

### CHAPTER III.

A Bed Puzzle—First Night at Sea—Doleful Experiences—Lights on the Norwegian Coast—The Pilot, . . . 24

### CHAPTER IV.

Bergen—Dried Fish—A Norwegian Sentry—The Fjeldvei—Strange Drinks—Hanseatic Museum, . . . 34

### CHAPTER V.

The Hardanger and Sör Fjords—Odde—Sandvenvand Lake—Buarbrœ Glacier—The Laatefos—The Oxen Mountain—Eide, . . . . . . . . . 43

### CHAPTER VI.

SS. *Miowera* — The Sogne Fjord — Balholm — The Nærö Fjord—Gudvangen, . . . . . . . 66

## CHAPTER VII.

Stalheim—The Zigzag Road—The Jordalsnut—The Stalheimfos and Sivlefos, . . . . . . . 79

## CHAPTER VIII.

Some Characters—The Exclusive One—The Early Morning Deck Promenader—The Perambulating Nuisance—The Kodak—The Wine List, . . . . . . 86

## CHAPTER IX.

Bakke—Öie—The Hjörend and Stor Fjords—The Geiranger Fjord, . . . . . . . . 99

## CHAPTER X.

Merok — The River Olga — Knuden—A Lemming — New Road above Merok—A Novel Conversation, . . 110

## CHAPTER XI.

Letters from England — Island of Lepsö — Molde — Its Church and Leprosy Hospital, . . . . . 123

## CHAPTER XII.

The Romsdal Fjord—Veblungsnæs and Aandalsnæs—Norwegian Ponies—The Romsdalhorn and Troldtinder—Hörgheim—The Mongefos, . . . . . . 133

## CHAPTER XIII.

The Hustadvik Headland — Christianssund—Trondhjem—Absence of Slums—Broken-down Bridge—The Lower and Upper Lerfos, . . . . . . . 144

## CHAPTER XIV.

Trondhjem Cathedral and Arsenal—Shops at Trondhjem—Homeward Bound — Christianssund — Molde — Aalesund—A Scramble, . . . . . . . 156

## CHAPTER XV.

Bergen Museum—Old Wooden Church at Fantoft—Ironing the North Sea, and the Result—The Tyne and the Custom-House Officers, . . . . . . 168

# A Yachting Cruise to Norway

―o―

## CHAPTER I

*Choosing a Holiday — Norway — Inland Tour or Yachting Cruise — Conflicting Opinions.*

WE, the Parson and the Lawyer, one evening in the month of June 1894, were discussing our annual holiday, with the assistance of our pipes and glasses of whisky and water. And here let it be mentioned, in order that no injury may be done to anyone's feelings, that wherever in this narrative we are said to partake of whisky and water, it was the Parson that took the water and the Lawyer the whisky.

The Parson wanted a holiday that would be interesting at night schools, young men's improvement classes, mothers' meetings and winter evening lectures; in short, a holiday that would be inexpensive and make itself generally useful. The Lawyer wanted a holiday that would, for a short time, separate him, like the Styx, from the law reports, counsel and the law courts; in short, a place where clients cease from troubling and the lawyers are at rest.

Our thoughts rambled promiscuously to the flowery land of the Mikado, the foreigner-hating and now much-defeated land of 'the heathen Chinee,' the sunburnt plains and glorious cities of India, and the pyramid-crowned land of Egypt. But after poring for an hour over the latest sixpenny atlas—the meeting was at the house of the Parson, who is chairman of the School Committee—and a year-old 'Bradshaw,' we reluctantly arrived at the conclusion that not even the fastest Atlantic liner or torpedo-catcher could go to any of the before-named countries and back in a fortnight, to say nothing of an hour or two for doing all the sights of Japan, China, Egypt or India. So we turned our thoughts nearer home, and the land of the Vikings, the fjords, mountains and waterfalls appeared to us to meet, most nearly, all our requirements. We have not, as may be noticed, referred to Norway as 'the land of the midnight sun," because we are at a loss to see why the midnight, or any other sun, should be appropriated by any one country.

Having decided to visit Norway, we arranged to make inquiries, from those of our friends who had been to that country, as to the best course to take so as to get the greatest amount of enjoyment with a moderate expenditure of time and money. The Parson thought he knew, or could get to know, half-a-dozen men and ladies who had braved the North Sea and survived, and the Lawyer fancied he might include amongst his acquaintance double that number. To this intelligent British jury we proposed to put the following questions,—

1. Whether it is good policy to join one of the many yachting cruises, and if so, which?
2. Or, whether it is better to book to some port in Norway, and afterwards wander about the country

at one's own sweet will? If so, to what port, and whither to wander?

3. Any miscellaneous information.

And then we parted, to meet again in a month.

On returning to his office, the Lawyer set a typewriter to work, and by return of post received a wholesale supply of neat little sailing cards, books of itinerary embellished with natty little photographs, and cabin plans of ships; each cruise being the best ever devised, and each ship faster and more comfortable than any other afloat. After a cursory glance at them, pressure of business compelled the Lawyer to throw them into a drawer, where they remained until the day on which he was to meet the Parson. Then the unanswered queries confronted him, and the dreadful possibility of the Parson's malediction smote him. He rushed off to consult a young friend of the medical profession who spent his vacation in Norway the previous year, and having obtained the more or less valuable advice presently mentioned, the Lawyer bundled all the sailing cards, books of itinerary and cabin plans into a bag, and set off to meet the Parson, with a feeling of self-satisfaction in that he had performed his duty, and so fulfilled England's expectation.

It also happened that the Parson, owing to various causes more or less remotely connected with parochial matters, combined, as the Lawyer thinks, with culpable procrastination, had not until the day he expected the Lawyer, obtained a scrap of information. So, in the afternoon of that day, the Parson called on a lady possessed of ample means and a spirit of benevolence equally ample, who had paid two visits to Norway.

In the evening, when pipes were lit and the water and the whisky decorated the table, the Lawyer produced all his sailing cards, books of itinerary and cabin plans, and then gave the doctor's advice, taken down verbatim as follows,—

'Don't you be fool enough to go on one of those yachting cruises. They're frauds. You book to Norway—Bergen or Stavanger—and then do your own. If you join a yachting cruise you will be herded together with two hundred or so other fools, for whom you don't care a dash, one-half of whom are intent on flirting with and, perhaps, marrying the other half. That don't suit me. Why, when I was staying at Odde, one of those big cruising steamers came in, and I shall never forget it. There was a simultaneous rush on shore of one hundred and fifty people, and presently they were scrambling for the forty or fifty carioles and other conveyances. Then those who had been lucky enough to secure the vehicles came by me in a long procession. The dust was something awful, I can tell you. No; you take my advice. Don't burden yourself with a lot of luggage; take an extra shirt and a pair of stockings in a knapsack, and walk through the country as I did. That's the way to enjoy yourself and appreciate the scenery. No blooming Noah's Ark! Ta! ta! Hope you will enjoy yourself. But you take *my* advice!'

Then the Parson read his notes of the conversation with the lady,—

'Are you going to Norway? Oh, you will enjoy it. It is a delightful holiday, and the scenery is really too grand and imposing for words. I have been twice, and I think I enjoyed the second visit even more than the first, and I should like to go again. Oh, yes, a yachting cruise is one delicious dream from beginning to end, except perhaps while crossing the North Sea. The first time I sailed on one of the Orient boats, and nothing could be more comfortable or better arranged. The second time I went on the *Midnight Sun*, and she is such a nice boat. And then there is the *Victoria*. Oh, certainly I should advise you to take a yachting cruise. You meet such nice people, and you appreciate the scenery so much more when you have sympathetic companions. You have no trouble about hotels, no discussions as to where to go, and no responsibility. Everything is beautifully arranged for you, and the *cuisine* is much superior to what you get at a Norwegian hotel. Oh, do take my advice, join one of the yachting cruises and you *will* enjoy it.'

Somehow we could not quite reconcile the opinions of the lady and the doctor. Perhaps there may be some way of doing so, only we were too dense to see it. They both agreed on one point—that Norway is delightful.

Then the Lawyer proceeded to read the different itineraries, and after he had been working at them for an hour or so, it occurred to the Parson to drop the observation that he could only be away two particular Sundays, namely the 12th and 19th of August. As the result of some further investigation we discovered that no boat belonging to the companies, whose books the Lawyer had been reading, sailed on the day we wanted to start. So he picked up another very natty little book, and read,—

'Det Bergenske Dam—Dam—'

'Steady! steady!' exclaimed the Parson.

Then the Lawyer made a plunge,—

'Dampskibsselskab—yes, that's something like it, Det Bergenske Dampskibsselskab and Det Nordenfjeldske Dampskibsselskab.' There would be no danger of any flirting on a boat of that line, as no lady would so far lose her self-respect as to cross the North Sea in a vessel belonging to companies bearing such names as those. 'Here we are, the steamship *Venus* sails from Newcastle on Tuesday the 7th of August on a a yachting cruise, visiting all the chief fjords of Norway. New boat, and, like all the rest, the best afloat. The best cruise ever devised, and an excellent *cuisine*, equal to a first-class hotel.'

So we decided to sail on the *Venus*, belonging to the joint companies with the unpronounceable names, which have the honour of carrying the Norwegian mails, and we determined to secure a state-room about the centre of the ship, so as to avoid as far as possible the oscillation of the North Sea. The English agents of the Companies are Messrs P. H. Matthiessen & Co., Newcastle-upon-Tyne.

# CHAPTER II

Bank Holiday Travelling — Lost Luggage — The *Venus*—Sailing from the Tyne—Feeding Arrangements on Board—Our Table.

ON Monday, the 7th of August, the Parson journeyed northward, and spent the night at the Lawyer's bachelor quarters, and the following morning we set off for Newcastle, in the highest spirits, which were much tried and lowered before we arrived at the end of our journey. We reached Leeds with comparative comfort, notwithstanding the Bank Holiday; but at that station, owing, as one official told us, to the Bank Holiday excursions, everything seemed to have gone wrong. The 2.10 express for York was not. One honest porter said it must have lost itself somewhere. After waiting over an hour there was no sign of it, and we then happened to discover, at an adjoining platform, a train bearing the signboard 'York. This, we were told, was a slow train, but we thought we had better be thankful for small mercies, and that a slow train was better than no train at all. So we caught up our impedimenta, big and little, and hurried round. No sooner was our movement observed by the forlorn passengers waiting for the missing train, than they, one and all, followed our example.

As we passed through Durham, its glorious cathedral and castle, lit up with the afternoon sun, burst into view and then quickly disappeared like some magnificent vision of the past. As we lost sight of them, the thought struck us both that we should not, in Norway, see anything to compare with Durham in grandeur or historic interest.

On arriving at Newcastle we hastened to the luggage-van to claim our luggage, and behold the Parson's portmanteau could nowhere be found. We searched every luggage compartment three times over in vain, and then we looked at one another. The Lawyer noticed that the Parson was mutely appealing to him to say something appropriate, something that would be equal to the emergency and yet not offend the sacerdotal ear too grievously. The Lawyer rose to the occasion and burst out in a most venomous tone, 'Dampskibsselskab.' Then our pent-up feelings were instantly relieved.

We interviewed an official at the luggage office, who at first steadfastly affirmed that if we had seen the aforesaid portmanteau put into the train at York, and we both did so, no power, either human or otherwise, could have extracted that portmanteau from that train until it reached Newcastle. It was only the Lawyer's pertinent question, 'Do you mean to call me,' etcetera, 'and also my saintly brother,' that brought that proud official to contemplate the possibility of the missing article having been taken out of the train by mistake at some intermediate station. But having once come down to that level, he set the telegraph to work with a will. Det Bergenske Dampskibsselskab ran a special train from Newcastle to the *Venus*, lying in the Albert Edward Dock, and this special started at six o'clock. Two trains from York were due at Newcastle before that hour, so we had some hope of recovering the wandering baggage. The Parson had a little handbag with him, but that, of course, only contained a few things he could easily have dispensed with, and all his most necessary clothing was in the lost trunk. While waiting for the next train, we drew up a list of absolutely necessary things to be purchased at the last moment as an outfit for the Parson, and it was astonishing how long that list kept continually growing.

When the next train from York steamed into the station, the Parson stood sentry at one end of the platform and the Lawyer at the other. The latter was unsuccessful, but on looking up he saw the Parson at the farther end of the train frantically waving his umbrella, and the Lawyer knew by the Parson's glorified countenance that all was well.

We found a crowd of 'Venuses' on an adjoining platform awaiting the special; a dozen or two ladies, and perhaps twice as many men. Surely, we thought, these ladies cannot have been made acquainted with the dreadful name with which they are to become associated! Being bachelors, we considered we knew something about ladies, and we felt confident that as soon as they became intimate with the terrible word, the majority of them would be dreadfully ill. On looking at them a little more closely, we noticed that one or two did look a little pale, as if they anticipated something very unpleasant.

Oh, that special train! It started pretty punctually, but just outside the station it came to a standstill. Then it recovered itself a little and crawled on for a few yards. Once more it stopped, and again proceeded at a snail's pace, until it met a number of boys and girls whom it appeared to know; and when they surrounded it crying, ' Chuck me a ha'penny, oh!' 'Chuck me a ha'penny, oh!' it seemed quite at home and stopped for at least a quarter of an hour. At last some of the passengers, growing desperate, and evidently being under the impression that the train was 'held up' after the American fashion, threw a few coppers on to the adjoining line. Immediately two or three dozen boys and girls were sprawling and struggling on the ground between the lines, to the great consternation of some of us. But we need not have concerned ourselves, as we were told that a train travelling at the rate of ten miles an hour over that part of the line was unheard of. At anyrate, the officials of our train regarded the children on the line with the greatest complacency. When the scramble was over and there seemed no prospect of any more coppers being squeezed from us, we were allowed to proceed, or at least to go backwards, then we turn off on another line, and after one or two more stops, we reached the Albert Edward Dock and brought up alongside the *Venus*, having taken about an hour and-a-half in travelling what we took to be not more than ten miles.

Our first impressions of the *Venus* were very favourable. She is a nice-looking boat, rather high at the bows and was in spick-and-span order. The officers were in uniform and the sailors wore dark blue yachting jerseys. The sailors soon hauled the piles of luggage on board, and it disappeared into the different cabins in a very short time.

The proper thing to do immediately after getting on board seemed to be to secure a good seat in the saloon for meals by placing a visiting card under the serviette ring. This essential, we, from ignorance, not modesty, omitted to do. We first found our way to our state-room in the centre of the ship, and we examined with much curiosity our little bedroom for the next thirteen nights. We were startled to discover that the temperature was—well, something much too high to be pleasant. This we attributed to the near proximity of the boilers, but we thought that when we were under weigh and the sea breeze blew in at the port-hole, we should be cool enough. While we were stowing away our luggage in our cabin, we saw through the port-hole that the ship was slowly moving away from the wharf. As we had not previously seen the Tyne, we hastened on deck and stopped there while we crept out of the dock; the steam whistle meanwhile hooting out in ear-splitting tones the boastful proclamation to all and sundry, that Det Bergenske Dampskibsselskab's magnificent steamship *Venus* was under weigh for Norway.

As we proceeded down the river, we were constrained to admit that even the 'coaly Tyne,' at least in the darkening twilight of a summer's eve (this is a poetical interjection by the Parson), possessed a certain picturesqueness for which we had not given it credit. In half-an-hour we were in the open sea, and then we suddenly became alive to the desirability of ascertaining what was going on in the saloon. We found that supper was in full progress, and nearly all the seats in the inner saloon were occupied. However, the portly head-steward found us places at his own table, and for the first time we looked round on the 'other fools' with whom we were to be 'herded,' as the doctor put it, for the next fortnight.

The typical Englishman, if he does not know the name and social status of anyone who may chance to sit beside him, is supposed not to speak, either from fear of demeaning himself by becoming too familiar with someone who may turn out to be his social inferior, or from dread of being politely but firmly requested to mind his own business. We venture to think this supposition is not now well founded. Probably it applied to a generation long since passed away, who considered that every foreigner, and more particularly every Frenchman, was formed by nature of some very inferior clay to that out of which the lucky inhabitants of these Islands were constructed. At any rate, we did not find that unpleasant trait to be conspicuous in any of our fellow-passengers, with one possible exception. The Parson found himself opposite one of his own cloth, with whom he at once negotiated a friendly alliance. The Lawyer exchanged notes with a tall young man on his left, whom we afterwards ascertained to be a lieutenant in the Royal Engineers. Besides these, there were at our table a doctor, the only one on board, and we treasured him accordingly as a scarce and valuable commodity, two genial Irishmen, who contributed in no small degree to the joviality of our table—may their shadows never grow less (of which catastrophe there does not seem much probability), and a Scotchman who possessed the best telescope on board. We do not know whether our fortuitous concourse was brought about by a beneficent chance, so called, or whether the head-steward was gifted with an intuition beyond his fellows and settled us all at his table; but, however that may be, the arrangement was a most satisfactory one.

Det Bergenske Dam - and - the - rest-of - it served the meals at the hours customary in Norway, that is to say, to quote from the Companies' itinerary :—

'Breakfast from 8 to 10 o'clock, consisting of hot and cold meats, with potatoes, bread, marmalade, etc., and tea, coffee or cocoa ; porridge when desired.

'Dinner at 2 o'clock, consisting of soup,

fish, joint, *entrée*, puddings or cakes, cheese, dessert.

'Supper at 7.30 o'clock, consisting of hot and cold meats, with potatoes, bread, marmalade, tea, coffee or cocoa ; porridge if desired.

'Tea and coffee are also served in the morning and afternoon.'

Our table were of opinion that it would have been more satisfactory if the 7.30 meal had been made the dinner, and the supper served at 1.30 as a lunch. We even went so far as to suggest the transposition, but naturally discovered that arrangements of such vital importance could not be altered without the sanction of the highest authorities.*

During supper there was only just sufficient motion of the vessel to let us know we were at sea, and it did not appear to incommode anyone. A man at our table was unfeeling enough to remark that probably it was the last square meal that several of those present would enjoy for thirty-six hours.

* We understand this change is to be made for the 1895 season.

The Lieutenant endeavoured to insure himself against the adverse influence of the sea by taking champagne with his supper. The rest of us contented ourselves with tea, coffee or öel—a light beer, resembling lager beer, but happily without a suspicion of garlic.

A lady of noble proportions, seated at a table not very far from us, in a moment when the buzz of conversation lulled, was distinctly heard to demand in a loud, determined, do-it-or-die tone,—

'Steward, have you any Scotch whisky on board?'

'Ya, ya,' replied the steward; which, being interpreted, means yes.

'Then bring me a bottle,' returned the lady.

The steward looked at her for a minute, as if uncertain whether he correctly understood the lady's English, and then departed, and a low but distinctly-heard titter fluttered round the saloon. The steward soon returned with the bottle, and, after drawing the cork, he deposited it beside the lady's plate as if it had been a bottle of claret. Our table watched that bottle with considerable interest, but, we hope, without appearing to do so. The lady partook of a very moderate quantity, and shortly after corked up the bottle and carried it out of the saloon with her. We then understood that it was intended as a medicinal remedy against the horror of the sea, and we admired the bravery of the lady but not her tact.

It was quite dark when we had finished supper, and we all adjourned to the deck for a stroll. The night was fine, but cloudy. We were surprised to find that although we were only about an hour's sail from the mouth of the Tyne, not a single light could be seen in any direction. Presently we noticed a little speck of light flicker for a few seconds on the port bow (as we understand the nautical expression is) and then disappear.

'Do you speak English?' inquired the Parson of the sailor on the look-out at the bow.

'No, I do not speak English.'

'Not speak English,' exclaimed the

Parson, 'why, you have just spoken in very good English.'

'I do not speak a word of English, sir, not a word,' the man replied, without the semblance of a smile, at which remarkable statement we all laughed.

'He don't understand English. He only knows them two sentences,' said another sailor who came to the assistance of his mate.

The second sailor explained that the light we had seen was that of a fishing boat which had hoisted her lantern as soon as she saw us, and had lowered it again. This sailor stated that he had served on board an English ship, and so had learnt the future universal language, as we British and our American cousins like to regard it.

# CHAPTER III

A Bed Puzzle—First Night at Sea—Doleful Experiences—Lights on the Norwegian Coast—The Pilot.

EUCLID has laid it down that the lesser cannot contain the greater, and we think he must have discovered this truth from sleeping, two in a cabin, on board a ship. At any rate we could not imagine a better proof of the proposition than the attempt of two men, both of whom can stretch about six feet from the tip of one fore-finger to the tip of the other, to disrobe simultaneously in the space of about a yard and a half square. So the Lawyer, who, like all his profession, is a man of peace, remained on deck for a quarter of an hour after the Parson had retired. At the expiration of that interval, he went to the cabin and found the Parson standing on the edge of the lower berth, deeply pondering the mystery of a Norwegian bed in the upper berth.

'Look here,' he exclaimed with righteous wrath, 'the bed is not made at all, and there is no top sheet, only a blanket.'

The Lawyer also perched himself on the lower berth and gazed at the offending bed. Under the counterpane was a nice blanket, folded in a cylindrical form, lying on the bottom sheet, which was properly spread. The Lawyer could not solve the puzzle any better than the Parson, but we soon decided to make the bed ourselves and dispense with the top sheet for the night. So we seized the blanket, and, when we unrolled it, behold! there was the missing sheet cosily reposing inside, like the meat inside a sausage roll. We spread the sheet and blanket in the orthodox fashion, and the Parson climbed into bed, taking the greatest precaution not to knock his head against the ceiling—no, we mean the roof, or whatever the top of the cabin may be called.

Then the Lawyer inspected the lower berth and found it contained a sausage roll just like the top one. Having spread this out, he quickly completed his preparations for the night, making, meanwhile, some very uncomplimentary remarks as to the heat of the cabin, switched off the electric light, and crept into his berth.

Did anyone ever sleep during the first night on board a ship at sea? We know that we did not, but perhaps we were rather unfortunate in having a cabin close to the engines. As far as we could ascertain, the next morning the eight men at our table did not get an hour's sleep between them. The heat of the cabin, the interminable 'dinker, danker,' of the engines, the indescribable feeling of being boxed up, and the motion of the ship kept us awake.

What fools we were, thought the Lawyer, while tossing from side to side, hour after hour, in sleepless misery, to chose a holiday of this sort when we might have had a fortnight's golf in Scotland or Ireland, with peaceful nights in comfortable, airy rooms and good-sized English beds. Strange to say, but perhaps it was not strange but only natural, that several, we think we may safely say the greater portion, of the 'Venuses,' during the long hours of that night were tormented with similar thoughts. But the day came at last, according to the usual custom of days, and the Lawyer rose early, enjoyed a most refreshing bath of sea water and then went on deck.

The sea air was delightful after the heat of the cabin, the sun was glistening on the water, and the boat had a gentle, rhythmic motion that was not unpleasant. The Lawyer, especially when he presently saw the stewards carrying hot coffee into the smoking saloon, began to think that perhaps after all a yachting cruise might not be such a dismal affair as it appeared in the night.

Oh! ye business men who are day after day condemned to sit at the same desk from morning to night, ploughing your way through the daily accumulation of work! Oh! ye ladies who encounter each day the terrible bogies of the dinner, the cook, the fishmonger, the butcher and the grocer, say, do not your hearts thrill with a delicious sense of relief at the prospect of a fortnight's freedom from your slavery, a fourteen days' respite from business and bogies!

The 'Venuses' gradually appeared on deck, one by one, and the morning salutations and congratulations on the weather were heard on all sides. By the time the Parson came up, the bell was ringing for breakfast. That bell deserves a passing notice, for it was quite an artistic production. It was made of brass and resembled, but was rather larger than, two champagne glasses, minus the stalks, placed face to face, and the clapper was concealed inside. It possessed a handle whereby it was shaken, and the sound thereof was most agreeable, as the steward marched round the ship shaking it vigorously; at least we began to think so after we had crossed the North Sea, and when the air of the Norwegian fjords had stimulated our appetites so that we were always hungry.

At breakfast the saloon was not nearly so full as at supper the preceding evening, and we were sorry to hear that the North Sea, even in its gentlest mood, had proved unkind to many of our fellow passengers, not only of the fair, but also of the sterner sex. Our table, however, were all there, some of them looking as if they had been up all night, but we were all able to do justice to the breakfast and to a stray joke or two connected with our struggles with the beds.

We spent the morning delightfully, lounging in deck chairs, chatting, reading and smoking, with an occasional stroll up and down the deck. A deck chair, the canvas of which had at one end been nailed to the wrong bar, and consequently the chair could not be set up, caused a great deal of amusement. A dozen men, one after another, puzzled over it and attempted to set it up, but failed ignominiously, to the great merriment of the bystanders.

We passed one or two vessels homeward bound, at too great a distance to excite much interest, but they afforded good objects for the Scotchman's telescope and the field glasses which many of the men carried.

The wind and the sea had risen slowly but

very perceptibly during the morning, and when we went below for dinner at two o'clock, the ship was rolling and pitching in rather a lively manner, so that many persons preferred the fresh air of the deck and no dinner to the hot atmosphere and the strong smell of eatables below.

The company at dinner was not a large one, and most of us were surprisingly anxious to return to the deck. The stewards did not seem to apprehend the gravity of the situation, and being apparently under the impression that as we had nothing to do all the afternoon we wished to linger as long as possible over dinner, they moved about with slow precision, and exhibited an amiable composure that amounted to absolute cruelty. As a matter of fact, some of us had a great deal to do that afternoon. So it came to pass that before the sweets were on the table, about half the company, the Lawyer amongst them, found that their appetites had failed them and withdrew. The Lawyer afterwards explained, by way of extenuating circumstances, that on looking round the saloon, he noticed several persons casting wistful glances towards the door, and as he surmised they were mutely crying out for someone to make the first move, and as he also felt he would be happier on deck, he rose from the table with solemnity and made for the door. His example was quickly followed by many sympathisers.

That afternoon deck chairs were scattered all about the ship, each occupied by someone in a more or less pitiable condition. The Lawyer found a quiet, secluded seat on the upper deck, behind the bridge, where, happily, he went to sleep for an hour or two, and towards the evening, as he was feeling squeamish although not actually ill, he procured a cup of tea and a biscuit and then sought the seclusion of his berth. The Parson professed to be not at all affected by the motion, and took a quiet nap in the smoking saloon.

The attendance at supper, when the fiddles were on the tables, was very meagre indeed. The Lawyer was not there, but came on deck again in the evening when we got into smoother water. About ten o'clock the captain pointed out to us some lights on the Norwegian coast, which many of us were very glad to see; and an hour or so later we saw a light flare up some little way ahead, and the steamer stopped to take up the pilot. Presently we could just make out the pilot boat coming towards us, and a wave brought it against the side of the ship with a crash that seemed almost sufficient to stave it in, while its sail caught on the rails of the upper deck. The pilot climbed up a rope-ladder lowered for him, the second mate released the sail, and in less than half a minute the boat was lost in the darkness. After this we retired to our berths and the Parson again made his bed after the English manner, but the Lawyer did not take the trouble. He insinuated himself into the end of the cylinder, and, finding it very comfortable, communicated his discovery to the Parson. Thenceforward we adopted this plan, and came to the conclusion that the beds, when treated in a proper way, were all that could be desired.

We slept better the second night, notwithstanding the heat, and were awakened about four o'clock the next morning by the noise of the anchor going down, and the working of the donkey engine. On looking out of the port-hole, we saw that the *Venus* was being moored alongside the quay at Bergen.

Our selection of a vessel, as will be seen, depended rather upon the date of sailing than any other consideration; but, judging from the result, we do not know that we could have made a better choice. The *Venus* is a nice boat, very handsomely fitted up, and we hope at some future time to enjoy another sail in her.

# CHAPTER IV

Bergen—Dried Fish—A Norwegian Sentry—The Fjeldvei—Strange Drinks—Hanseatic Museum.

WE heard that several of the passengers were not sailing for the entire cruise, but were leaving the ship at Bergen, so, immediately after breakfast, we interviewed the second mate with the object of changing our cabin. We were fortunate enough to secure a cabin further forward, away from the engines, and which also had the advantage of a ventilator in the passage just opposite the door; and we may here mention that we were as comfortable in our new cabin as it is possible to be on board ship. We were pleasantly cool at night, and were no more troubled with sleeplessness.

After moving our belongings, we set out with the Lieutenant to see the town, the Lawyer having Baedeker's Guide in his pocket. The *Venus* was moored to the quay, almost opposite the castellated tower built in the middle ages to overawe the merchants of the Hanseatic League, who inhabited the quarter now covered by the red-tiled blocks of buildings called the Tydskebryggen adjoining the harbour. We had to pass these buildings in order to reach the town, and when we came near them an overpowering smell of dried fish smote us. The word 'smote' is not a shade too strong; in fact it scarcely satisfies us. The sun was very hot, and as we hurried along the five hundred yards or so up the Tydskebryggen, the stink was simply terrific. We glanced in at several open doors and up the passages, and found that the houses, warehouses and courtyards were piled as full as they could hold with stacks of dried fish. There must have been millions of them, and each fish appeared to be doing its very best to augment the general volume of smell, which we felt was likely to have the same effect on us as a very rough sea. We hastened on, and it was a relief to us to leave those fish behind and enter the wide main street of Bergen.

The houses are built almost entirely of wood, and are picturesque and clean, many of them showing signs of having been recently painted. The windows of the shops in the principal streets were artistically arranged, and seemed especially designed to extract the money from the pocket of the British visitor. We were told that in nearly every shop one or more of the attendants spoke English, and, with the usual impudence of our race, whenever we walked into a shop we took it for granted that we should be understood. We entered the quaint old church called the Korskirk, which, however, has not much to boast of in the way of architecture or internal decoration.

After leaving the church, the Lieutenant discerned in the distance a sentry marching up and down in front of a building, and he at once started off at the rate of five miles an hour to hold an inspection. The light blue uniform of the sentry, which might have fitted a much larger man, the funny little arrangement he wore on his head, which seemed a cross between a helmet and a bowler hat, and his slouching walk, evoked the contempt of the Lieutenant.

We made our way to the Fjeldvei, a new road winding up the face of the Floifjeld Hill. This road, we were informed, was constructed out of the profits of the drink traffic in Bergen under a system very similar to the Gothenburg. We climbed up a very steep zigzag path, taking many rests by the way, for the sun was very hot. After about an hour's climb we reached the highest part of the road, and by the side of it, a little further on, we saw a small châlet or refreshment room. Thinking that a lager beer would be refreshing after our exertions, we attacked the châlet, but found it locked up and deserted. A few hundred yards up the mountain stood another châlet, and reaching this we seated ourselves in a verandah overlooking Bergen. A small boy appeared, and in answer to our inquiry for lager beer shook his head. We then asked for soda water, milk, whisky, but the imperturbable boy again solemnly shook his head after each word. As a last resort we mentioned ginger beer, and immediately a smile lit up the boy's face, and he went out. He soon reappeared carrying a tray, whereon were three black bottles, resembling half-pint claret bottles, three glasses and a corkscrew. The Lawyer drew the three corks, and the liquid in the first bottle was white, the second bottle contained a fluid of a deep yellow colour, and the third bottle a rich crimson concoction. The different colours caused us much amusement, and the three glasses looked like the coloured jars in a chemist's shop window. The white drink tasted of apples, and we voted it the best of the three; the yellow was flavoured with oranges, and the crimson, we thought, with raspberries. And all these drinks appeared to figure under the name of ginger beer! But perhaps the boy did not understand us, and brought us samples of all the liquors in the establishment.

A lady and gentleman who crossed with us in the *Venus*, but were now going inland, came into the châlet, and to our amusement asked the imperturbable boy for milk and soda, then for lager beer, and were answered by a shake of the head, at which stage we interfered and recommended the white drink.

The view from the châlet was exquisite, and quite worth crossing to Norway to see. Bergen lay below with its red-tiled roofs and white houses, and its harbour full of ships of all descriptions. These, with the beautifully blue water of the fjord and the brown, barren mountains beyond, combined to form a picture we shall not readily forget.

We dined that day at two o'clock, the usual Norwegian hour, at the Grand Café instead of on board the *Venus*, and had an excellent dinner. It rained heavily in the afternoon, so we waited at the café for an hour or two after dinner, hoping that it might clear up. But as there did not seem much prospect of it, and we were to spend another day at Bergen on our return from the fjords, we decided to go back to the *Venus* and look at the Hanseatic Museum on the way.

This museum is located in one of the old houses in the Hanseatic quarter. The house faces the wharf, but the entrance is a few yards up a passage or narrow street. We mounted the outside wooden steps leading to the door, which is at the end of a little balcony, but found the door securely fastened. Two ladies and a child were sitting in the balcony close to the door, and observed our unsuccessful efforts. Just as we turning away in disgust, one of the ladies pulled a bell which we had not noticed, and after a few minutes' delay, a young man opened the door. As soon as we had all entered, he spoke to the ladies in Norwegian, and we understood him to ask whether they were Norwegians. On their replying in the affirmative, he told them they need pay nothing. He then turned to us and inquired our nationality in English, and asked us to put a krone each into a box. Eighteen kroner are the equivalent of one pound sterling, an ore is the hundredth part of a krone.

The museum consisted of four or five rooms, just as they were inhabited by a Hanseatic merchant about two hundred years ago; and in the rooms were various articles of more or less interest belonging to the same period.

Amongst them were an old ledger containing a great number of entries relating to shipments of goods, principally to ports in Germany—we could not find the name of an English town; a kettle, various tools, two or three swords of rather inferior workmanship, two hide whips about two feet long for chastising the apprentices and others, for which purpose they would be most effective, a few pictures and chairs, an old brass font, which particularly attracted the Parson's attention, and a few other miscellaneous articles. The small cupboard-like beds, resembling berths on board a ship, in which the occupants of the house used to sleep, were perhaps the most interesting objects. We were in the house about half-an-hour, and as it was very hot and stuffy we were glad to get out, but on the whole the inspection is well worth a krone. Perhaps we should mention two dried fish hanging from a beam across the ceiling, represented to us as being two hundred years old at least, and which, by the way, did *not* stink. The different articles were very well described and their use explained by the young man, first in Norwegian to the ladies and then in English to us, or *vice versa*.

After leaving the museum, we had to run the gauntlet of the fish, which we did with as much expedition as was consistent with our dignity and the heat. The *Venus* was to stop a day at Bergen on the return voyage, and it was suggested that we should purchase a supply of eau-de-cologne as an antidote to the fish, but we feared the scent would be overpowered and utterly vanquished in the unequal contest. Happily we discovered that an electric launch ran, from a little jetty close by the *Venus*, to the other side of the harbour every few minutes, and by crossing in the launch we could get into the town very comfortably without encountering the smell.

# CHAPTER V

The Hardanger and Sör Fjords—Odde—Sandvenvand Lake—Buarbrœ Glacier—The Laatefos—The Oxen Mountain—Eide.

As soon as supper was finished, the *Venus* sailed southward for the Hardanger Fjord, and just as she got clear from the quay she fired a salute with her four little brass guns. The salute was returned by the ss. *Mira* belonging to the Bergenske Dampskibsselskab, which happened to be entering the harbour at the moment, and the sound of the eight guns went echoing about the mountains. When most of us were endeavouring to work ourselves up to a full appreciation of the grandeur of the noise, the scientific Lieutenant was energetically sniffing the smoke made by the discharge, and then he disenchanted us all by exclaiming that 'it was dashed bad powder,' in a tone that led us to believe he considered himself to be professionally insulted by the use of a very inferior article.

The rain had ceased and we were treated to a really glorious sunset. The clouds near the setting sun were bright gold, and surrounding these were heavier clouds of a deep rose colour, gradually fading into a pale pink overhead, while the east was pearly grey. We stood on deck watching the beauty of the slowly-changing sky, and the mountains and hills on each side of the fjord, some jagged and barren, others clothed from the base to the summit with small pine trees, which seemed to perch themselves wherever there was a cranny large enough to hold a handful of soil.

After it became dark, we remained on deck, standing in the bow with the sailor on the look-out, and observing with much interest the lights that beaconed the fjord. As each light came into view, the vessel appeared to steer straight for it until another light appeared, sometimes straight ahead, sometimes to the right or the left, and immediately our course was altered for the succeeding light. Suddenly the sailor turned towards the bridge and shouted out something in Norwegian, which he afterwards interpreted to us as meaning 'A steamer on the port bow.' We strained our eyes in that direction, and presently made out the light. It proved to be a fjord steamer belonging to one of the allied Norwegian companies, and very pretty she looked as she went by, with her saloon and deck illuminated with the electric light.

When we awoke the next day, we found the *Venus* was at anchor at the end of the Sör Fjord, close to the little village of Odde. It was a lovely morning. The mountains on each side of the fjord were so high and precipitous that the *Venus* lay in the shade, but we could see the brilliant sunshine lighting up the tops of the mountains to the west.

At breakfast our table decided to visit the Buarbrœ Glacier in the morning and to drive to the Laatefos Waterfall in the afternoon. We were rowed ashore in the *Venus's* boats, and some of us who were rather lazy drove in stolkjarrer—small two-wheeled pony carts with a seat wide enough for two moderately-built persons and a little perch for the skydsgut or driver, behind—to the Sandvenvand Lake; but others, including the Parson and the Lawyer, walked. As it was uphill nearly all the way, and the skydsgut very properly will not hurry his pony uphill, those who walked arrived at the lake, which is only about a mile from Odde, a few minutes after the others who drove. The first arrivals, however, secured all the boats at the Odde side of the lake, and we sat down disconsolately and saw them gradually growing smaller in the distance. We lit our pipes and tried to persuade ourselves that perhaps after all the glacier was not worth seeing, and that the lake was the more interesting object. Presently we observed a little line of smoke creeping across the lake towards us, and on a more particular inspection we discovered that a small boat appeared to be connected with the smoke. Surely, we thought, it must be a small steam launch. And so it proved to be, and as it drew near we hailed it with much satisfaction. When we started across the lake in the launch, the boats seemed to us to be close to the other side; however, after about ten minutes' steaming, to our surprise, we overhauled the boats, one after another, and found that they were not much more than half-way across. Their progress was slow, as they had to contend against the current caused by the river which runs into the lake at the Gaard Jordal village. Distances in the clear Norwegian air are very deceptive, as we found on this and many subsequent occasions.

We landed at least ten minutes before the first boat arrived, and started up the valley. We could see the glacier a little way ahead, and considered we should easily get there in half-an-hour. The path ran along the side of the river, a sort of mountain torrent, tearing along at a splendid rate, foaming and roaring over the boulders and stones scattered about its course, and making such an uproar that, when close to it, we had to shout to make ourselves heard.

We followed the path at a fair pace,

winding round rocks and boulders, passing through little pine woods, crossing miniature streams and waterfalls, but always ascending upward. Every small open space of ground had been recently mown for hay, and looked like an English lawn, studded, however, with little wild flowers—blue, yellow and red—just such as may be seen in England, only many more of them, while the hay was hanging on the curious hurdle arrangements to dry. Every quarter of a mile or so we came to a wire attached at the lower end to a rudely-constructed windlass, the other end stretching far up into the mountains on one side or the other of the river. It was suggested by one of our party that these wires were fixed for the purpose of permitting the trees growing in the valley to inquire of the trees high up on the mountain 'whether it is cold up there?' after the manner of the small boys in the street accosting a tall man. If it were not for the pleasure afforded by the wires of making this polite inquiry, it was feared the little trees in the valley would die of envy. The natives also utilise the wires for sliding down from the side of the mountain bundles of grass and brushwood, but of course that is quite a secondary matter.

On and on we plodded for half-an-hour, a whole hour, and still that deceptive glacier looked just as near as when we started, but not a bit nearer. The sun was hot and the uphill work made us very warm, and if it had not been for the refreshing coolness of the wind caused by the icy temperature of the river, we fear some of our party would have voted the glacier a deception and given up.

'Baedeker' told us that there was a farmhouse on the path, where refreshments could be obtained, and although we carefully looked out for it, we could see no human dwelling of any sort. However, after about an hour and twenty minutes' walk, we came to the top of a rise, a little steeper than usual, and there, a short distance in front, on the other side of the river, stood the farm. A bridge led to it, and on our side of the bridge was a large board with the word 'Restuation' painted in big black letters. We do not know whether this was intended to be an English word or not, but the meaning of it was clear enough. We hastened on and soon seated ourselves in the cool parlour or kitchen, we are not sure what title it lays claim to, of that most welcome farmhouse. Here we waited about a quarter of an hour, and then, refreshed by lager beer and the rest, we proceeded to the glacier, first pausing to admire a little waterfall at the back of the farm, which crept over the top of the mountain like a small silver band, and fell in fussiness and froth and foam by the side of the outbuildings, where it was made to turn a grindstone. It seemed indignant, as many men and women are, at being compelled to work in order to pay for its way, and as it passed the troughlike shoot—which it endeavoured to avoid as much as possible—it hissed out its denunciation of the shameful invention of labour in no measured tones.

About a couple of hundred yards from the farmhouse, and something like the same distance from the glacier, was a patch, half an acre or so in extent, of oats, which had been cut, tied up in small sheaves and impaled on poles fixed upright in the ground.

At last we stood at the foot of the glacier. From the bottom of it issued the river, rushing and seething as if it had just tumbled over a considerable fall. The end of the glacier was indented with several chambers or crevasses, some many yards deep, and in these the ice assumed a beautiful bluish-green tint.

It was the first time that some of us had seen the mighty force, which we are told has performed such herculean tasks in scooping out valleys and levelling hills on this earth, and accordingly we began to insult it and show our contempt for it by throwing stones at it, endeavouring to break off projecting pieces, and poking it with our sticks. But it regarded all our efforts with supreme contempt. It spoke to us in a dignified tone, as plainly as a creature without lungs can speak, and said,—' Look well at me, ye puny animals, whose short existence is but a day. A hundred generations of your race have

I beheld; yea, before man appeared upon this earth I was here. After you are dead, hundreds of succeeding generations will behold me here. Silently and slowly, yet surely, I fulfil the eternal laws of the Almighty and accomplish the work that He has committed to me. Go ye, and learn from me uncomplainingly to do His will, and ye shall find rest at the end of your days.'

On the way back to the lake we met several 'Venuses,' and they all inquired how far it was to the glacier, and seemed astonished that they had not already reached it. About half way up we came upon the lady of noble proportions, and a gentleman of proportions scarcely less noble, sitting on a rock by the side of the path, evidently somewhat exhausted by the walk up. We had the satisfaction of assuring them that 'Restuation' was not far ahead.

The walk back to the lake, being downhill, seemed much shorter than the climb up. When we reached the half-a-dozen small shanties forming the village, we were accosted by a man in a highly-excited condition, who demanded,—'Are you English?' We assured him we were, and expressed the hope that the knowledge of our nationality might afford him every satisfaction. 'Thank heaven!' he exclaimed, in a tone of great relief, as if the fact of our being Englishmen was to him of the utmost importance. We expected some very startling intelligence to follow, or at least an urgent appeal for a loan, but he merely asked,—' Have you seen a boy carrying a bag as you came down from the glacier?' We restored his peace of mind by assuring him that we had seen several boys with bags or wraps. From the experience gained during several little jaunts abroad, we sometimes think that the most curious people met with out of these islands are either Englishmen, Irishmen, or Scotsmen.

The steam launch again bore us across the lake, and we drove down to Odde in stolkjarrer, the ponies trotting down hill as fast as they could put their feet on the ground. The pace seemed a trifle dangerous, as there were two or three sharp turns in the road, and a precipitous drop on one side of it. A skydsgut has not the slightest objection to trotting down hill, and appears to put the greatest confidence in the surefootedness of his pony, but we did not put much trust in the harness.

After dinner we again landed and engaged a stolkjarre for the drive to the Laatefos Waterfall. The road as far as the lake was the one we had traversed in the morning, and the skydsgut and we walked up the hill to ease the pony. We skirted the lake for two or three miles. The road in some places was cut through the solid rock, and there was generally a drop of from ten to twenty feet on the lake side, with no continuous fence, but merely large stones, about three feet high, placed a yard apart, considerately leaving just sufficient space for anyone who felt so disposed to take a header on to the rocks below, without first having the trouble of climbing over the stones.

Before leaving the lake, we passed a

waterfall, which, if situated in England, would be considered something stupendous, but as it is overshadowed by the magnificent Laatefos, the drivers do not usually stop, and we only bestowed upon it a passing glance. While looking at this comparatively insignificant waterfall, we noticed that clouds were gathering round the tops of the mountains ahead, and almost immediately it began to rain. Luckily we had our mackintoshes with us.

After leaving the lake, the road runs by the side of a river, which in some places is a rushing rapid, and in other parts broad and tranquil like a small lake. Presently we heard a noise resembling thunder ahead, and suddenly the Laatefos came into full view. The road crosses a bridge in front of the fall, and the spray comes over the road in sheets, but as the rain was also coming down, not merely in buckets-full, as the saying is, but in hogsheads-full, we were only able to distinguish the spray from the rain by the direction from which it came.

We pulled up on the further side of the bridge, and hurried up the winding path to the small hotel, in front of which the best view of the fall is obtained. We carefully picked our way to a projecting rock, just at the spot where the immense mass of water in the further fall takes its last leap into space, and here we stood for many minutes lost in contemplation at the indescribable grandeur of the scene.

Then we made for the hotel, and found it full of dripping 'Venuses'—some having tea and others endeavouring to rid their clothes of a little of the superfluous moisture. Here we saw the two Irishmen who had driven up a little way behind us, and had brought no overcoats or waterproofs with them; consequently they were in just such a state as they would have been had they taken a bath with their clothes on.

Notwithstanding our waterproofs, we were very damp in places, and the Lawyer thought a little whisky would help to keep away a cold. He was very doubtful whether such a thing could be obtained, as it is generally understood that these establishments are not allowed to sell intoxicants; but he ventured to ask the young lady in attendance if he could have a dose of whisky medicinally, as a preventative against a chill. The damsel glanced at him in quite a professional manner, as if to ascertain whether he were a fit subject for medicine, and apparently having satisfied herself that he was, she retreated into an adjoining room, and returned with a bottle of Scotch whisky and a liqueur glass. She filled the glass, and triumphantly handed it to the Lawyer, who humbly asked if he could have a little water and a tumbler. The young lady opened her large brown eyes to their widest extent, gazed up at him with amazement, and exclaimed, 'Water!' She had evidently never heard of whisky-and-water, and the Lawyer reflected that there could be no School Board in Norway, or, otherwise, this young creature would not have been permitted to remain in such dark heathen ignorance.

As no water or larger glass seemed to be forthcoming, the Lawyer took his medicine neat. His little manœuvre was quickly observed, and then there was a simultaneous rush of dripping humanity towards that young lady and her whisky bottle. The Lawyer waited not to see the full result of his evil example, but, conscience-stricken, fled, forgetting not first to pay half-a-krone —or was it a krone?—for his physic.

The Laatefos followed us, and poured down upon us all the way back to Odde— at least the water that fell on us resembled the Laatefos rather than ordinary British rain. When we reached the ship, we looked as if we had swum on board, and we hastened below to change everything.

The *Venus* was timed to leave Odde at six o'clock, but, as a number of the party did not get back until at least an hour later, the Captain considerately postponed our departure until we had finished supper, so that we might not miss the beautiful scenery of the fjord. We may here mention that, throughout the cruise, Captain Oxholm did everything in his power to promote the comfort and enjoyment of the passengers.

As we threaded our way down the fjord, we were treated to glimpses of the gigantic Folgefond on the tops of the mountains to the west. The Folgefond is an enormous field of snow and ice covering the plateau from three to five thousand feet above the sea, extending from north to south upwards of twenty miles, and varying in width, from east to west, between three and nine miles. The rain had ceased, but clouds were still drifting along, and sometimes we could see the base and top of a mountain while the centre was veiled by a broad band of mist.

The summit of the Oxen mountain was shrouded in thick clouds, so that we could not appreciate its full proportions. However, it looked very majestic, towering up until lost to view. There was quite a little gale of wind blowing up the Hardanger Fjord, and we hoped it would disperse the clouds and reveal to us the Oxen's head when we returned from Eide. The Oxen is not a difficult mountain to climb, and we are told that from the top of it a splendid view of the surrounding mountains and fjords can be obtained.

As we turned into the Graven Fjord, at the end of which the village of Eide is situated, we passed an immense cliff, forming one side of the Oxen and rising straight out of the water to great height. It was suggested that this cliff might, if taken in a scientific method, be used as an antidote to Bristol-Suspension-Bridge-suicidal-mania, and the recipe was elaborated as follows,—' If any unfortunate man'—and in this recipe, as in Acts of Parliament, the masculine gender includes the feminine—' has deliberately arrived at the dismal conclusion that the suspension bridge, or other violent means of exit from this world, is the only thing that is left for him, then let him adopt the following course. Let the unfortunate scrape together, by hook or by crook, sufficient funds for a journey to Norway. Let him look forward with enthusiasm to the voyage across the North Sea and to the beautiful and romantic—as the guide books say—mountains and fjords. Let him determine and fully convince himself that the last week of his life shall be one of uninterrupted, pure enjoyment, and cast off as an old coat all the troubles which have combined to reduce him to such a desperate state of mind. Let him refrain from overdoses of strong drink, and keep from it altogether if he possesses not sufficient strength of will to stop when he has had enough. Let him endeavour to spend his last week in pure appreciation of the beauties of Nature, including that of his fellow creatures, and, after arriving in Norway, if his funds will allow, let him stand for half an hour beside the Laatefos, visit the Buarbrœ Glacier, and any other place that may interest him. Then, if his fell determination still remains, let him make his way to the Oxen and struggle up the mountain until he gains the head of the cliff, forgetting not to pause many times on the way to breathe the pure mountain air, and to admire the glorious view of mountain, water and sky. By this time his liver will have resumed its normal functions, his troubles will appear insignificant, and life once more worth living. His rash, premeditated act will be banished for ever, and he will return home a more contented and happier man.' This may seem like the Parson's sermonizing, but in justice to him we must say it is not.

When we had passed the Oxen, the *Venus* appeared to be heading straight for a mountain, and we could not see any possibility of an opening. The mountains ahead were arranged in a semi-circle, and apparently formed an impenetrable barrier, but still the *Venus* sailed placidly on as if trusting to Providence to cleave a watery way through miles of rock. One man confidently asserted there could be no outlet, and it was suggested to him that he should so inform the Captain. Presently the mountains ahead appeared only a few hundred yards off, and it looked as if we must run ashore in a few minutes. Then a little cleft was seen to the right—we beg pardon, we mean the starboard—and this, as we rounded a projecting rock, widened out into a broad fjord. A repetition of this experience is constantly happening while sailing up the fjords, and the direction in which the boat is to emerge from what is apparently a watery *cul-de-sac* is a source of continual speculation, not of money, but of mind.

It was dark when we reached Eide, so that we could see nothing of the place except the lights in the distance. A few of the passengers left the *Venus* here in order to travel overland by Vossevangen to Stalheim, where they would again join the steamer. After studying our itinerary, we decided to remain on board, because we did not want to miss the sail up the magnificent Sogne Fjord, and Nærö Fjord, which we had heard so much lauded, and we found we should have time to visit Stalheim from Gudvangen.

The *Venus* only stopped at Eide long enough to disembark one boat-load of passengers and their luggage. Then she swung round and steamed back down the fjord on her way to Bergen and Gudvangen. The Oxen was still wearing his night-cap when we re-passed. We thought it would have been more polite of him had he doffed it to us, especially as we had ladies on board.

'Why on earth are they making such a row on deck!' were the words with which we both started up about four o'clock the next morning, and after a moment's reflection we realised that the unearthly racket was caused by the lowering of the anchor. 'Why can't they,' we growled, or at least the Lawyer did, 'let us have our sleep in peace and run the ship quietly ashore, or do something or anything that would not make such a confounded noise!' And then the donkey engine commenced its rasping rattle and clatter, loud and harsh enough to be heard ten miles off. It appears to us that the chief object of a donkey engine is to create the most horrible din, and that the manufacturers of these machines must have this particular in view as the most essential feature of their productions. We cannot conceive any arrangement of wood or metal that would give forth more discordant sounds with an equal expenditure of power. We, as bachelors, have been told that a year-old baby with healthy lungs is able to do a good deal as a disturber of rest and destroyer of peace, but it is not in the same street—to use a vulgar, trite expression—with a donkey engine. It would be futile to mention how many times during the cruise we mentally consigned our persecutor to the deepest abyss in the North Sea. We believe there are five of these pests reposing on the deck of the *Venus*, but it was the one in the bow that raised our deadly hatred by disturbing our sleep. The others were comparatively inoffensive creatures; some of them were covered with canvas and served as seats.

In about an hour or so, just as we had succeeded in getting to sleep again, the donkey engine re-commenced its braying and we re-commenced our grumbling. Happily we were not long in getting under weigh from Bergen wharf, and then we had peace for an hour or two, until an early riser began to promenade the planks just above our heads.

# CHAPTER VI

SS. *Miowera*—The Sogne Fjord—Balholm—The Nærö Fjord—Gudvangen.

WHEN we went on deck after breakfast, the morning following our rest-breaking call at Bergen, the *Venus* was steaming up the coast, within the chain of islands, in smooth water. The mainland, as seen from the ship, consisted of hills of no very remarkable height, and chiefly barren. Rocks and islands innumerable studded the seaward side, and on some of them were small clusters of cottages, others were pictures of craggy desolation.

The Captain told us that we should probably meet the ss. *Miowera*, which had had the misfortune to run on a rock about seventy-five miles north of Bergen a few weeks previously. We remembered reading in the papers that she struck the rock at night, when all the passengers were in their berths, and we can well imagine their consternation and dismay as they rushed on deck in all sorts of *déshabillé*. The Captain had heard at Bergen that the *Miowera* had been floated off the rock and might be expected to enter that port during the day. She came in sight soon after, attended by two tugs, one in front and the other astern. She was a fine boat, painted slate colour, and we gazed at her with much curiosity. Above the water she did not seem much the worse for the accident, but we were given to understand that below the water-line there was a great rent in her bow, which had been temporarily covered over. We gave her a cheer as she steamed slowly by, and the officer on deck acknowledged the salutation by raising his hat. Of course there were no passengers on board, they having been taken back to England by one of the Norwegian mail steamers, a few days after the tragic termination of their cruise.

Towards noon we entered the Sogne Fjord,

and the scenery gradually became more imposing. It was a lovely morning, with bright sunshine, and a gentle breeze just sufficient to ripple the blue water. We thoroughly enjoyed ourselves, basking in the sun on the deck, smoking and chatting, and revelling in lazy appreciation of luxurious idleness and freedom from all responsibility. The fjord is a grand watery highway with an average width of four miles, but in the clear atmosphere and with the aid of field-glasses or the Scotchman's telescope, the farms and cottages on both sides could be clearly seen. We passed several picturesque little homesteads, perched high up on the sides of the mountains in almost inaccessible spots, and many quaint little villages in the valleys, some possessed of a miniature church, plainly distinguishable.

Early in the afternoon we came to Balholm, a lovely place, situate at a bend of the fjord, with a few neat-looking villas and a large hotel.

'What a beautiful little retreat for a honeymoon!' exclaimed a pretty young lady, in whom we took an especial interest, because we fancied her husband and she had been lately initiated in the bliss of holy matrimony; but our little romance was rudely shattered when we afterwards discovered that she was a young matron of two years' standing.

A lady and gentleman wished to disembark at Balholm, and as soon as the *Venus* stopped two or three hundred yards from the shore, a number of boats put off and raced towards us. When they came near, we noticed with amusement that all the rowers were children under ten years old, and there were two in each boat. One boat was *manned* by two small girls, and another by a girl and a boy. The girls did not win the race, for two boys reached our gangway first, and the boy and girl crew were a good second. In a few minutes half-a-dozen boats were crowding round the gangway, and the miniature seamen and seawomen were shouting at and pushing one another, until the second mate intervened and ordered them to keep clear of the ship. One boat was selected by the gentleman, but when the lady and he got into it, they and the two boys quite filled it, so that the boat with the boy and girl crew was taken to carry their luggage, and they made for the shore followed by the disappointed youngsters in all the other boats. Then the *Venus* fired a grand salute from her four guns; but, alas! the fourth gun missed fire at the first attempt, and the dramatic effect was spoiled and turned to burlesque, as the laugh of the bystanders testified. The smoke drifted slowly astern in a little white cloud, and one large circle, such as some would-be-clever young men delight to blow from their mouths when smoking, but much greater in size and volume, floated away by itself and was visible for some minutes rotating in the clear air.

On we sailed through ever-changing scenery, all the sunny afternoon; mountain after mountain, valley after valley, waterfall after waterfall succeeding one another in endless variety, like the monotonous yet ever-delightful cadence of some beautiful poem.

At length we entered the Nærö Fjord, and the mountains became loftier and more precipitous, the fjord narrower, the waterfalls larger and more numerous, and we were lost in wonder at the indescribable beauty and grandeur of the scene, which, when once seen, will never be forgotten, but, in the words of Shelley, will be a 'joy for ever.'

Just at the entrance of the Nærö Fjord, at the foot of a high mountain, was a small patch of ground, perhaps twenty square yards in extent, unapproachable except by water, and on this tiny plot was growing a flourishing crop of potatoes. Someone must have considered it worth while to row a long distance to till this tiny garden, and we mention the circumstance to show how the frugal Norwegian folk utilise every available yard of ground.

About four o'clock we reached Gudvangen at the end of the fjord, and dropped our anchor a short distance from the land. Looking backward, we appeared, owing to a bend in the fjord, to be in a land-locked lake, surrounded on all sides, except where the village lay, by mighty mountains, rising sheer up in almost a straight line several thousand feet, over which, in many places, silvery streams of water fell, breaking into white froth and spray as they struck the first projecting crag in their downward course, sometimes hidden from view for a distance by an outstanding rock, and again appearing lower down, until at last they found rest in the quiet waters below.

The boats were soon lowered and most of us went ashore. About six of our table took a walk along the path, or road, as we believe it is called, running back from Gudvangen by the side of the fjord to a little village called Bakke, which we had noticed when steaming up the fjord. The road in places is cut through the rock by blasting, and we could see the borings in which the explosive had been inserted. Some ponies were grazing on the scanty grass at one place where the mountain at its base was not precipitous but rose for some distance in a slope much steeper than the roof of a house. One pony left the road in front of us, and scrambled, like a goat, up a steep ascent that would have been a good climb for us, until it reached a patch of grass where it commenced grazing. Small wild flowers and ferns were growing in crevices among the rocks, and wherever a handful of soil had clung after falling from the top or side of the mountain. Two or three times during our walk we heard stones or small pieces of rock fall two or three thousand feet, clattering against each jutting ledge and rattling down on to the stony *débris* at the foot.

One of our party, but neither the Lawyer nor the Parson, was looking forward with much joy to entering shortly into wedded felicity, and he began to dig up some fern roots to take home to his lady-love. Then we poor, miserable, unappropriated wretches thought that although we had no fair one who was all in all to us, yet we had some lady relations who would be glad of fern roots from Norway; so we followed the happy one's example and began digging up ferns with our sticks. How many of those roots reached England we should scarcely venture to say. We fear that most of them, like good resolutions, were forgotten, or fell victims to the confined space of the staterooms. Only two or three of ours survived, and these have been planted with care, and are now watched with much interest by the recipients.

While the Lieutenant, the Parson and the Lawyer were lingering behind the others, devoting their attention to the ferns, a little animal, somewhat smaller than an English field-mouse, darted out from under some stones close to us, and began running too and fro over a mossy piece of ground, sticking his snout, in shape something like a pig's, into the moss just as a dog hunting a rat might do. Suddenly he appeared to find his game and then commenced digging in the moss with his snout, all his four feet scratching at the same time with astonishing rapidity. Every muscle of his little body was strained to the utmost to get at the tiny quarry, and the excitement and energy displayed by the diminutive creature was most comical. He was successful in capturing the article he was in search of, and he paused a moment to eat it. Then he started hunting again, darting backwards and forwards within the space of two square yards, and soon found another interesting spot, when the digging operations were repeated with the same excitement and activity. We stood quite close to him and stooped down to have a nearer inspection, but he took no notice of us whatever, and was not in the least afraid. He was not more than two inches long, without measuring his tail, and was of a light fawn colour. Probably he was quite a common little animal, but very uncommon in being so tame. We shouted to the others to come back and see this beastie; but they were too far ahead, so we left him and followed them.

Soon after this the *Venus* fired her guns, and the effect in the deep fjord was remarkable. The sound reverberated from side to side, ever higher and higher up the mountains, until it appeared to reach the summits, when it lost itself in space. The smoke slowly drifted towards the other side of the fjord and clung to the base of a mountain like a small cloud. Apparently it was heavier than the atmosphere, and therefore did not rise.

Further on we came to a waterfall, not large in volume but descending from a very great height, and we climbed up the stony slope until we reached the foot of the fall. Here we sat down on some rocks and watched the water dashing, splashing and whirling down, close beside us. We tasted the water and found it icy cold, owing, no doubt, to it having just descended from the perpetual snow-field at the top of the mountain.

Sitting at the foot of the fall, there was not a living thing in sight, except a greyish-black crow, which started from the rocks above us and flew across the fjord to the mountains on the other side. We watched it becoming smaller and smaller as it fluttered on and on, and upward towards a high cliff, until it became like a pin's head in the distance, and then was lost to sight.

Of course, here we ought to have reflected on the wild, solitary grandeur and romantic nature of our surroundings. We should have speculated on the character of the gigantic convulsions of the crust of the earth, which had millions of summers ago reared these mighty mountains, and of the never-ceasing but slow action of the glacier which may have cut the deep fissure now forming the fjord. We should have quoted appropriate verses from Scott, Byron, Tennyson and Wordsworth in praise of the beauty and charm of the mountain and lake, the sky, flowers and waterfall. The appropriated one should have unconsciously breathed a sigh as he thought of his fair maiden across the sea, beneath another sky, and we should all have sighed in unison. In a novel we should, no doubt, have done all these things. But, alas! we did not. One of us began to try if he could throw a stone into the fjord some hundred feet below, and all the rest basely followed his example.

On our way back to the *Venus* we looked out for the sporting little digger, and sure enough we found him not far from the same spot. He was still busily engaged in his important duties, scratching away every now and then as if his whole existence depended on his exertions. We concluded that he must be working for a small wife and big family concealed somewhere in the rocks, and we pointed him out to the engaged one as a terrible example of the hard lot in store for him after matrimony. Suddenly the little animal appeared to become aware that six bigger animals were surrounding him, staring down at him and making impertinent remarks on his proceedings, so he promptly decamped and took refuge under a rock. May he sleep peacefully through the long Norwegian winter, and wake up again next spring as sprightly as ever!

# CHAPTER VII

### Stalheim—The Zigzag Road—The Jordalsnut— The Stalheimfos and Sivlefos.

THE following day was Sunday, and the Parson, accompanied by another parson, interviewed the Captain, and arranged for a service to be held on board at five o'clock in the afternoon. There is no church at Gudvangen, but there is a small one at Bakke. We were told, however, that a service was held there on alternate Sundays only, and not on that Sunday, so we arranged to drive to Stalheim in the morning. The rectitude of our consciences (especially the Lawyer's) compel us to say that we should probably have taken the drive just the same, even if there had been a service at Bakke, but we mention the excuse as it reads so nicely.

Five of us engaged a light, open carriage, drawn by a pair of stout ponies, and set off soon after breakfast. The road from Gudvangen to Stalheim runs, as most Norwegian roads do, by the side of the river, rising in places fifty feet or so above it, and at others sinking almost to the level of the water. We had to go up and down several rather steep but short hills. We invariably walked uphill for the sake of the ponies, and all rode downhill, often at a gallop. At several places the road for a few yards resembled the bed of a water-source, and was covered with round stones varying in size from a golf ball to a cricket ball. We alighted at these obstacles, and it was as much as the ponies could do to drag the empty carriage through. Our skydsgut happily could speak English, and told us he had been employed as a groom in Yorkshire for two years. The Lieutenant rode on the box during the drive out, and before we arrived at the bottom of the ascent to Stalheim, he had gained enough information from our skydsgut, who had served in the army, to enable him to write a treatise on the Norwegian military system. At least we gathered as much from his subsequent learned observations, which the rest of us listened to with unprofessional humility.

We passed here, as in many of our drives in Norway, plantations of small bushy trees, the leaves and twigs of which we were told are cut, not to make brooms or articles for whipping naughty boys, but to be stored up to serve as fodder for the cattle in the winter. Whether this is a true tale or no, we know not, but we scarcely think the trees can be grown for the especial benefit of the boys, because the former far out-numbered the latter, and two trees for one boy would be too terrible an idea. Is it possible that they treat the girls the same as the boys in Norway?

The river was beautifully clear, and looked as if it ought to hold some nice trout. Boulders and rocks were strewn along its bed in happy confusion, and over and round them the waters surged with a ripple and gurgle that was most delightful and refreshing in the hot sun.

The scenery is a continuation of that of the fjord—lofty mountains, more or less precipitous, rising each side of the river, and conspicuous amongst them, on the right, stands the giant, round-headed Jordalsnut. We have not so far mentioned the height of any mountains, because we find the guide books vary considerably in that particular, and, also, we think that when on a holiday, figures and statistics are obnoxious to most people, except when they occur in connection with dinner time or the wine list.

At the bottom of some of the cliffs we saw dead trees lying, mixed with earth and large boulders, which our skydsgut told us were the result of avalanches in the spring.

In about an hour and a half, we arrived at the bottom of the steep, zigzag road leading up to the top of the pass. Here we left our conveyance, and proceeded up the hill on foot. The *Venus* being due to leave Gudvangen at noon, we were rather pressed for time, and hurried up one zigzag after another, hoping and believing that each one was the last. However, there seemed an endless succession of them, and from each one we could only see the one immediately above. Eight, nine, ten and eleven were passed, and we thought that a dozen would surely complete the number! But no, twelve and thirteen were negotiated and fourteen appeared ahead. Here several of our companions stopped, but others, including the Parson and the Lawyer, pushed on. Fifteen and sixteen were passed and seventeen loomed above, eighteen came in sight and at last, at the turn, we rejoiced to get a splendid view of the magnificent waterfalls, the Stalheimfos and the Sivlefos, and, a little further on, at the head of the pass, stood the hotel. We had taken about twenty minutes coming up, and our knees were aching smartly as we sat down on an accommodating boulder and gazed round at the glorious array of mountains on every side. Their summits, some round, others jagged and in places white with snow, stood out clear against the sky, while colours of many shades could be seen in their barren or tree-girt sides and dark crevices, as the sunlight played upon some parts, and others lay in deep shadow. The view is truly a very grand one, and we rested for a quarter of an hour or more, regardless of our limited time, looking first in one direction and then another, and at each glance fresh beauties revealed themselves.

This is generally considered to be one of the grandest views in Norway, and so far as our small experience goes, we quite coincide with that opinion. We very much wished we could have spent a day or two at the hotel, and could have seen the mountains in the early morning and evening light. Possibly on some future occasion we may have that treat. However, it was a bright, sunny day, and we consoled ourselves with the reflection that, probably, no conditions of weather could have been more favourable.

We took several short cuts on the way down, which, unlike many so-called short cuts, helped us considerably. It was half-past twelve, however, before we got back to the *Venus*, but such were the attractions of Stalheim that there were many later than ourselves. The Captain blew the whistle to hasten them, and about one o'clock we started down the fjord.

# CHAPTER VIII

Some Characters—The Exclusive One—The Early Morning Deck Promenader—The Perambulating Nuisance—The Kodak—The Wine List.

WE propose in this chapter to give a short sketch of some characters, specimens of which, more or less developed, were on board the *Venus*, and we think are generally met with on a yachting cruise. It must not be supposed that we are alluding to any particular individuals, but rather to types. We are told on good authority that 'the proper study of mankind is man,' and although the feeding arrangements, and the scenery, especially the former, occupy a good deal of time and attention, yet one's fellow-passengers are always near at hand, and the opportunities of observing their peculiarities are unlimited.

First of all we will mention 'the exclusive one.' This gentleman, we do not call him a man, or he would be seriously offended, possesses such an extravagant idea of his own importance that he scarcely condescends to speak a word to anyone on board except the Captain. To make use of an old expression, it would be a good commercial speculation to buy him at another person's valuation and sell him at his own. He endeavours to cultivate the Captain, because he likes to pose on the bridge and strut from side to side in the orthodox seaman's fashion, free from the contamination of the inferior clay below. He is always found there when the scenery is particularly attractive, and if any other person ventures to intrude on the sacred spot he regards it as a breach of his prerogative.

When not on the bridge, he generally takes a deck chair and places it on the upper deck, close to the front rails, so that his supercilious eyes cannot be offended by the sight of anyone in front of him. There he studies his 'Baedeker' or reads a novel, but never passes a remark, or allows the doings of his fellow passengers to interest him in any way. In fact, he does not appear to see them, his eyes seem to be constructed peculiarly, or perhaps, from constant habit, have acquired the singular property of not reflecting and transmitting to his brain the pictures of men and women whom he may consider not to be equal, or superior to himself, in social standing. But if he can buttonhole anyone who is remotely connected with the peerage, or a well-known public man, then he is quite transformed. His reserve at once disappears, he becomes painfully affable, and his ungenial laugh is heard repeatedly. This man never smokes. He knows nothing of the soothing influence of the sweet-smelling weed, or of the sympathy existing amongst smokers. His self-imposed solitude is never alleviated by the companionship of a favourite pipe, and he is never seen in the smoking-room, which to him would be a sort of purgatory. We do not know whether 'the exclusive one' ever went on shore, but we suppose he must have done so occasionally, although the Norwegian skydsgut, who treats his fare on terms of absolute equality, and likes to shake hands at the end of the drive, would scarcely be to 'the exclusive one's' taste. We are glad to say there was no example of this pronounced type on board the *Venus*, but on another cruise, which shall be nameless, there was a very advanced specimen. We could almost bring ourselves to pity this gentleman, did we not remember that he was himself solely responsible for his isolation. One would like to suggest that he should give up his exclusiveness, should renounce his belief that he is so much superior to the ordinary run of humanity, and if he sank many degrees in his own estimation he would rise considerably in the opinion of other people.

It is amusing to notice the different costumes on board. Here we have a man got up in a light-coloured shooting or golfing suit with white gaiters, evidently a new rig out, and he seems very proud of it. In a day or two he discreetly drops the gaiters, which seem rather out of place on board ship.

Then there was another young man, one of our table, whose little weakness it was to appear every other day or so in a different suit. We began to count them, and we believe there were seven altogether. How he managed to stow them away in his state-room was a mystery. Most of the men on board had just a change or so, in case they should get wet through, and these, with underclothing, dressing-gown, overcoats and miscellaneous articles were quite sufficient to fill the limited space available for baggage in the cabin.

'The early morning deck promenader was voted a terrible nuisance. Every morning about six o'clock, when all the other passengers were sleeping below, he appeared on deck, shod in thick boots. Then with fiendish malignity he commenced a quick promenade right round the deck just above the heads of the would-be sleepers beneath. Round and round he went with clockwork regularity, and his heavy, jarring tread, every three minutes, came nearer and nearer, passed right overhead, making more noise than a dozen dinner bells, and then receded, only to return again and again. Many times the Lawyer felt sorely tempted to rush on deck and pitch 'the early morning deck promenader' overboard, and then return to his berth feeling that he had done a praiseworthy act for the benefit of his fellow-sufferers.

We believe the fiend, after effectually waking up everybody, and causing no end of wicked words to be breathed from what would otherwise have been the most innocent of lips, would appear at breakfast and boast of the beautiful early morning walk he had enjoyed on deck, and the grand appetite he had thereby gained, while the rest of us were asleep! Forsooth, as if sleep were possible during his selfish circus performance!

We occasionally suffered from another perambulating nuisance of a much milder form. This was a rather wild-looking, lantern-jawed young man, who believed that the prolongation of his valuable life depended on his taking a daily constitutional walk of several miles. In the afternoon, when the deck chairs were spread all over the ship, and the occupants were enjoying themselves smoking, reading, or taking a quiet nap, then 'the perambulating nuisance' saw his opportunity and promptly seized it. He began to walk briskly up and down, wherever the legs and toes of the sitters were thickest. As he came near, feet and legs had to be withdrawn and huddled up under the chairs to make room for him to pass, for he was not at all particular to occasionally kicking or treading on anyone's toes, hastily apologising as he proceeded, but, of course, never pausing for a moment in his most important duty. As soon as he had gone by, legs were stretched out again, only to be drawn in as he re-passed. This continued until somebody was bold enough to move his chair so as to entirely block up the way, and then when 'the perambulating nuisance' came up to the obstruction, he stopped for a moment and looked at the offending barrier and those sitting near with the air of a long - suffering martyr defrauded of his birthright, and as if he regarded with superior and almost tearful pity the selfishness and want of sympathy which some persons exhibited. Then he would turn away with a little shrug of his shoulders, and restrict his peregrinations to the other portion of the deck.

One man incurred the maledictions of those occupying cabins near his, and at the same time excited their pity. This was a rather stout man with a constitutional cough of great harshness and penetration. It generally used to come into play in the early morning and continue with slight intermission until breakfast. Very often the 'early morning deck promenader' and the cough were both in full swing at the same time. Probably the promenader started the cough, so we could sympathise a little with the latter. However, when both were performing in concert, rest was quite out of the question, and the best thing to do was to accept the inevitable, take a bath, dress, go on deck and enjoy a cup of coffee and a biscuit.

The Kodak, especially the lady Kodak, might, we think, on some occasions develop into a terrible bogey, but although there were several on board, they were used with praiseworthy discretion. Next time we sail on a yachting cruise, and may it be soon, we mean to furnish ourselves with a Kodak, not only for its legitimate use, but as an admirable means of self-defence. Hath not Scott sung :—

> 'The hunting tribes of air and earth
> Respect the brethren of their birth.'

And shall a Kodak on the prowl dare to attack a brother Kodak? We trow not. Besides, we should have felt great satisfaction in catching and fixing for ever 'the exclusive one,' 'the early morning deck promenader,' 'the perambulating nuisance,' and at least one fair one in whom we took an interest and also all the jolly companions of our table, who, alas! will never meet all together again in this world.

The *Venus* possessed a very fair wine list, and as the wine had not, we believe, paid English import duty, it was sold for much less than would have been charged for it at an English hotel. The Lieutenant did our table yeoman service in exploring the wine list, and, in fact, the head steward and one of his assistants were generally occupied for ten minutes at least, at the commencement of every dinner, in searching for the brand the Lieutenant had selected; meanwhile the rest of our table were deprived of the head steward's services. This happened time after time, until it became a joke, and whenever our steward was absent, we took it as a matter of course that he was after the Lieutenant's wine. However, we all shared, to a certain extent, in the benefit of his investigations, and so did not grumble, at least not much.

Some of the wine was kept in lockers at the end of the saloon, close to the stern of the ship, but the main store was in a well-like cellar, about eight feet deep, under the saloon, from which it was entered by a trap door in the floor. The assistant steward had to explore this cavernous depth at nearly every dinner, and on one occasion, just as his head appeared at the top, he slipped and fell with a crash of broken bottles. Two or three of our table got up from their seats, and, on looking down, found that the man had cut his wrist rather badly. He was trying, unsuccessfully, to bind it up himself with his handkerchief and would not come up, so he was taken by the arms and hauled out, and then he hurried out of the saloon with our doctor after him. Happily, the damage did not prove to be very serious, and he was on duty again the following evening. This was the only accident that occurred on board during the fortnight, either amongst the passengers or crew.

The doors of the cabins were generally kept open at night on account of the heat, and a thick curtain, provided for the purpose, drawn across the doorway. Early one morning, just as it was getting light, the Parson, who was awake, saw a hand and arm come in underneath the curtain of our cabin, and grope about the floor in a most mysterious manner, as if seeking for something. At the time, the Parson could not account for it, and wondered what the arm and hand were supposed to be doing, waggling about in our cabin. It appeared that the appendage belonged to the stewardess, and that she was seeking for our boots, which, as we had been wearing brown ones, we had not put out to be cleaned. The Lawyer did one night set his brown boots outside the cabin door to be polished, and the stewardess in the dim morning light must not have noticed the character of the boots, for, when he next saw them, one boot was brown and the other was black. We heard that the arm and hand entered the adjoining cabin in a similar fashion, and the occupant, who was somewhat of a wag, inquired what was the matter. The stewardess, from outside the curtain said, 'Shoe;' and the man, who did not like his rest disturbed by wandering arms and hands, shouted out 'Shoo,' which although probably not understood, had the desired effect.

# CHAPTER IX

### Bakke—Öie—The Hjörend and Stor Fjords—The Geiranger Fjord.

WE seated ourselves on the upper deck as the *Venus* got up her anchor, and leaving Gudvangen astern, steamed back down the Nærö Fjord. Picturesque little Bakke again came into view, its miniature white church decorated with a somewhat ambitious spire, standing close to the fjord. This tiny village, nestling in its romantic valley beside its foaming river, and hemmed in at the rear by mighty, hoary-headed mountains, is indeed a charming spot, at least in summer. In winter we can imagine the villagers could tell a different story. After passing Bakke, the narrow fjord and precipitous cliffs seemed to us even more impressively beautiful than on the preceding day. We were told that the Geiranger Fjord, which we hoped to see on the morrow, was still more stately and imposing, but we could scarcely believe it.

Just as the *Venus* entered the Fjoerlands Fjord, the welcome sound of the dinner-bell drew every one down to the saloon. During dinner we occasionally glanced out of the nearest port-hole, and could see that we were passing close to lofty mountains; but as it was a case of choosing between dinner and the scenery, we are ashamed to confess that no one was æsthetic enough to forego the material pleasure—or shall we say duty—of the table for the beauty of nature. Before dinner was finished, the *Venus* had steamed up the fjord and down again, so that the only view we had of it was a very cursory glimpse through the porthole. Possibly the pilot on the bridge and the few sailors on duty enjoyed the sight for the hundredth time, but, if they did not, then was a considerable amount of steam and time wasted.

The service at five o'clock, in which four of the clergy on board took part, was a great success. Nearly every passenger was present, and the time-honoured prayers of our ancient Liturgy never sounded more impressive, and the glorious old hymns were never more heartily sung than by that little congregation floating down the broad waters of the Sogne Fjord. One's thoughts travelled home to England, where numberless congregations had breathed the same words that day, and, further still, to the loved ones who had reached the last quiet port to which we are all steering.

We retired rather early that evening, as we felt we wanted a good night's rest, and we were successful in obtaining it. All night long the *Venus* was speeding northward up the coast, past the celebrated sea-cliff, Hornelen, rising straight out of the water nearly three thousand feet, which we have read about, but did not see; past the Nord Fjord, which we were not to visit; round the storm-swept Stadt headland outside the chain of islands, where the rolling and pitching of the ship woke us both up early in the morning. However, we suffered no inconvenience from the motion, but were soon asleep again, and did not wake up until the noise of the anchor going down at Öie, and the footfall of the early morning promenader, effectually roused everybody.

We went on shore immediately after breakfast for a stroll through the village, which boasts of one fair-sized hotel, two or three shops, and half-a-dozen houses and cottages. Like all Norwegian villages at the ends of the fjords, Öie seems to subsist on the tourist's gold. The shops display their wares for him, the hotels are built to accommodate him, and he alone finds employment for the numerous carioles, stolkjarrer, skydsguts (we apologise for the English plural) and ponies.

Öie is surrounded by mountains very similar to many others we had seen in Norway. One, however, has a peculiar, divided peak, and a deep gash down its side, as if it had been slashed with a sword and time had not closed the gaping wound.

We had here the opportunity either of driving across to Hellesylt and rejoining the steamer there, or of remaining on board and sailing back up the Hjörend Fjord into the Stor Fjord, and then up the Sunelvs Fjord to Hellesylt. Some of our table took the overland route, but we thought the fjords were the most attractive. The distance across is only about eight miles, the road being a very rough one.

The *Venus* sailed from Öie at ten o'clock, and we, with three others of our table, settled ourselves comfortably in deck chairs on the starboard side, near the bow. It was a beautifully bright morning, and the heat of the sun was tempered by a fresh breeze. We were provided with 'Baedeker' and 'Murray,' smokes of various descriptions, and novels, and we laid ourselves out to enjoy another day's delicious sailing. What though the Hjörend and Stor Fjords might not be quite so magnificent as the wonderful Naerodal, yet they presented many charming pictures of still waters, ragged and precipitous cliffs, mountains occasionally topped with snow, and waterfalls too numerous to mention, besides many beautiful effects of sunshine and shadow, sky and cloud. Could we not watch the seagulls, wheeling round and round, every now and then swooping down to dip themselves in the fjord, or to secure some morsel of food, and rising again without an apparent effort; sometimes following the vessel for miles. Could we not cast glances now and then at three pretty girls, gracefully lolling in their deck chairs a few yards off, just opposite us, on the other side of the ship? Were not two of them fair and one dark, so that they appeared more beautiful by contrast, and in order that the taste of each of us might be duly respected and satisfied? And did not a friendly gust of wind scatter over the deck some loose papers belonging to the dark sister, and give one of us the welcome task of collecting them and handing them back to the fair owner? And did not this result in an interesting conversation all about nothing in particular, yet very absorbing and entertaining? What more could any young man born of woman require to render a morning absolutely delightful.

So the hours sped away, all too quickly, until, soon after one o'clock, we reached the village of Hellesylt at the end of the Sunelvs Fjord. Here we found our friends who had journeyed overland waiting for us, and as soon as they were on board we started for the renowned Geiranger Fjord. Hellesylt is a small place, proud of the possession of a wooden-built church, conspicuously placed on a little hill, and an hotel; and a very peaceful, pretty retreat it looks. Wars and rumours of wars, political and social commotions might shake the nations of Europe and threaten them with bloodshed and ruin, yet one would imagine that this quiet hamlet would remain undisturbed, that its inhabitants would continue to watch the morning sun gild the tops of the mountains, and listen to the music of their river as it flings itself down the rapids into the fjord, in blissful ignorance and unconcern, as if they were in another world.

The Geiranger Fjord opens out from the Sunelvs Fjord a few miles from Hellesylt, and as we had been led to expect such great things of this fjord, we were all in a state of eager anticipation. Unfortunately, it began to rain; but although unpleasant, the rain did not detract much from the grandeur of the scene. The fjord is a narrow gorge between immense mountains, which in some places are absolutely precipitous and bare of vegetation, and in others rise in a very steep slope, the upper parts being thickly clothed with pine trees. Over the lofty cliffs several waterfalls splash down into the fjord, almost losing themselves in spray before the bottom is reached, but the volume of water in each fall is not great. We understood we should see seven falls close together, called the Seven Sisters, but two of them must have been 'not at home' when we passed, as we only saw five. These were not very imposing, the quantity of water being small. They were, however, very picturesque, creeping over the top of the cliff, three thousand feet or so above us, like bands of silver, and widening out and sending forth foam and spray as they slid down the side of the rocks and struck against and encircled each projecting crag, until at last they dashed into the waters of the fjord. The cliffs in some places had very curious black bands or streaks running down them, which everybody likened to ink spilt over the top, only a small river of the useful black fluid would have been necessary to effect the result. Owing to the winding course of the fjord, it frequently happened that, on looking ahead and astern, the vessel appeared to be completely land-locked. As the *Venus* steamed slowly along the narrow, dark waters, beneath the stupendous cliffs, it was impossible not to feel impressed with the solemn magnificence of the surroundings.

One of the mountains was quite precipitous at its base, but half way up it ran back for some distance in a slanting direction, apparently almost as steep as an ordinary house roof; and on this slope was perched a farmhouse, round which we could see several small bright green fields where the hay had recently been cut, and encircling the fields were thick plantations of pine trees. Above the slope, the mountain rose in a nearly perpendicular line, and the dark young lady and the Lawyer, as they gazed at the elevated homestead, could not see any possible means of access to it, unless the occupants had discovered the art of flying, or had provided an immensely long ladder to climb up and down. We have since ascertained that there is a ladder-like path, made accessible with the aid of irons and chains fixed in the rock; but how cattle or ponies could be got up to the farm is a mystery. Possibly the only live stock consists of goats.

The fjord near its termination widens out into a broad circle, and just at the entrance to this amphitheatre, as the guide books call it, the cliff on the right-hand side assumes the shape of an old-fashioned three-decked pulpit, no doubt by far the most ancient in existence; but the architect has omitted to provide the stairs for the preacher to mount to his lofty stand. If this rock had been situated in the imaginative East, what wonderful and weird legends of the past, and awful prophecies of the future would, in the lapse of centuries, have become associated with it!

At the further end of the amphitheatre stands the village of Merok, and here we dropped anchor, not far off our old friend the *Mira*, whom we were constantly meeting unexpectedly.

# CHAPTER X

Merok—The River Olga—Knuden—A Lemming—New Road above Merok—A Novel Conversation.

As soon as the anchor was down at Merok, dinner was announced, and we negotiated it as quickly as the gravity of the occasion and the pleasure of the stewards allowed, and then went on shore. Merok is somewhat larger than the ordinary run of fjord villages, and possesses several hotels and a peculiar church, built in the shape of an octagon, standing on high ground. We tried to enter the church, but found the door locked, and as we did not know where to apply for the key, and did not want to waste any time in making inquiries, we continued our walk. The guide books told us that a splendid view could be obtained from a point called Knuden, five and a half kilometres from Merok, and we made for that place. The road all the way there is one long, steep hill, so we decided to use our own legs and not give a poor pony the trouble of dragging us up. Besides, a young doctor who had joined us wanted to do a little climbing, and there appeared to be plenty of scope for it here. The road winds and twists backwards and forwards up the mountain, something after the fashion of the road to Stalheim, only the zigzags are longer, more numerous, and perhaps not so steep. In places the road ran for two or three hundred yards in one direction, and then turned and crossed about twenty yards or so higher up. Instead of following the road, we climbed straight up the mountain in several places, from one turn of the road to another, and by this means we left far behind us the carioles and stolkjarrer, in which many of the 'Venuses' were being hauled up at a slow walk. At one point, where the road took a very long slant, we must have saved at least a mile. In this instance, however, we were afraid we should have to retrace our steps, for we could see the mountain stream between us and the road above, and we were debating whether we should try to wade across it or ignominiously go back, when to our delight we found a rough bridge a little further on which served our purpose beautifully.

This river, the Olga, descends from the mountains in a succession of rapids and cascades, and is seen sometimes on one side of the road, sometimes on the other, rushing and splashing along its rocky way at a great speed. After again joining the road, we came to another hotel, the highest at Merok, from the front of which a splendid view of the fjord is obtained. Some little way further on, a path to the right, with a signboard by it, leads to an outlook at the edge of the precipice, commanding a very fine prospect of the Storsaeterfos Waterfall on one side, and, on the other, of Merok down at the bottom of the valley, many hundred feet below.

On returning again to the road, we came,

in a few minutes, to a precipice several hundred feet deep, at the edge of the road, on the right-hand side. A rather weak and shaky iron fence alone prevents anyone from slipping over, and it seemed to us that if a cariole, owing to some mishap, ran against this protection, the conveyance and its unfortunate occupants would take a flight of hundreds of feet on to the rocks below.

A few yards past this spot we noticed a little animal lolloping along on the grass at the side of the road in a very leisurely fashion, and on getting close to it we found it was a lemming. We had seen a dead one on a former walk, but had not previously made the acquaintance of a living specimen, and this fellow was very much alive. When we got up to him, he stopped and erected his nose as if to ask 'What the old gentleman we wanted with him?' We put a stick close to him, and he flew into a terrible rage, showing his teeth and swearing furiously. Then he attacked the stick, but finding that his teeth did not make much impression on it, he appeared to think that swearing was his most effective weapon, and recommenced with redoubled energy. We wanted to see him run, but he preferred to stand still and swear. At last, by giving him a touch behind, which interfered with his dignity, we persuaded him to take a few steps. His pace, however, was so slow that we could quite understand his objection to show off his deficiency in that respect. He stopped after travelling about three yards, and began scolding again. He did not wish to run away and escape; he evidently wanted to fight. We did not satisfy this wicked propensity, but left him, and no doubt he prided himself on having defeated four monsters each a hundred times as large as himself.

We saw numbers of these quaint little beasts further on, and they are very common in some parts of Norway. They have brownish stripes on the back, and are white underneath. *Nuttall's Diction-*

*ary* informs us that they are nearly allied to the mouse and rat, but they have sadly degenerated from their allies in the matter of speed and agility. A fairly active mouse would give a lemming ten yards' start in fifteen, and beat him easily; and would not the lemming stop and swear sweetly when he saw the mouse pass him! To outward appearances, the lemming, with his short tail and broad body, seemed to us to resemble a diminutive guinea-pig more closely than any other creature.

A stolkjarre caught us up while we were engaged with the lemming, and the skydsgut, who was walking, saw another lemming, and killed it with a pat of his hand that would not have disconcerted a rat in the least.

Half a mile or more beyond the precipice the road turned to the right, and we quite thought we had reached the top of the pass. We were mistaken, however, for we could see that the road, after a level run of two or three miles, again continued its winding course for several miles up a much higher portion of the mountain. The carioles and stolkjarrer, several of which had now passed us, all stopped at a little shanty dignified by the before-mentioned name of Knuden, not much beyond the top of the first ascent and in sight of the second; but as the *Venus* did not start from Merok until two o'clock the next morning, the Parson, Lawyer and Doctor determined, if the light would allow, to push on to the top of the next ascent. All the rest of our companions returned to Merok.

We walked along the road for two miles without seeing a human being, and not a single house or cottage was in sight. A road more desolate and wild than this, after the shanty at Knuden is left behind, we do not know. We did at length meet a man and woman who presented a curious appearance. The woman was without any hat or cap, and her hair fell down her back nearly to her waist. She wore a black gown of ordinary type, and this seemed to make the hair arrangement look the more peculiar. If she had been dressed in native costume, we should not have thought her primitive fashion so glaringly out of place. The man had on a rather seedy black suit, and he was possessed of a bowler hat. A woman walking along a mountain road, many miles from any habitation, minus any head-gear and with her hair down, was to us a novel sight.

We inquired of this strange couple how far it was to the top of the pass. The woman replied in a language we did not recognise, and then we began searching for a tongue both parties could understand. English and French were of no service, but we found that German was indifferently spoken and partially comprehended by each side. The woman, however, became most dramatic, and her energetic dumb language was highly entertaining. She threw her arms violently above her head, accompanying each movement with a little jump, in order to illustrate to us the immense height we had to climb before we reached the top of the pass. And then she began to laugh at her own antics, and the comicality of the whole proceeding was so intense that the whole party began to laugh uproariously. Altogether we had a lively and amusing interview, and we separated with great good-will after shaking hands all round. We think both parties considered the conversation to have been a great success, although the amount of intelligence exchanged was very small. The only information we gained was that the road ran up the mountain in front of us for a long distance, and that we could see for ourselves.

At length we came to the bottom of the second ascent, and by following very ill-defined paths up the side of the mountain from one bend of the road to another, we saved a long distance—the climbing, however, was pretty stiff work. We plodded on, sometimes along the road, sometimes up a rough track, until we reached the last zigzag where the road turned to the right and appeared to cross the top of the mountain range about a mile ahead. Here we held a consultation, and as it was seven o'clock, and we had no provisions with us, and could not get any nearer than Merok, we determined not to go any further. We rested a short time at the elevated spot, and thoroughly enjoyed the deliciously cool air and the wild desolation of the view. Merok was far out of sight at the foot of the first ascent, ten or twelve miles away, and we could not see a building of any description, and no living thing except a few goats browsing amongst the rocks to the right of us. We understand that the road has only been constructed within the last half a dozen years, and it certainly possesses great attractions for any one who admires a wild and unfrequented landscape.

We walked back in the cool of the evening, putting on our best pace so that we might get some supper at one of the hotels. The downhill journey was a pleasing contrast to the climb up, and we were somewhat hungry before we reached Merok, having eaten nothing since two o'clock.

A short distance from Merok we met the dark young lady and her two sisters taking an evening stroll, and a little way behind them their brother, a young clergyman, who was hurrying after them. He asked us if we had seen a bear, because he had just passed some Germans who had come down from Knuden in front of us, and one of them raised his finger and said to our friend, 'Beware—a bear!' Evidently the German was having a little joke at the expense of our countryman.

The landlord at the hotel had supper ready for us in a very short time, and we thoroughly enjoyed it. Here we first tasted the raw, dried salmon so much eaten in Norway, and, contrary to the experience of most people, we liked it.

From the hotel window we could see the *Venus* lying in the fjord below, and while we were satisfying the inner man, we heard our old friends, the brass guns, give tongue.

Then the *Venus* blazed out with a fine display of rockets, red and blue lights, and Roman candles. This incited the proprietor of the hotel to light up, and he set red and blue lights burning at each end of the grass terrace in front of the hotel, overlooking the fjord, and stationing himself in the centre, he fired off a Roman candle. Altogether, what with the fireworks on the water and on the shore, we could imagine we were at some pleasure resort in England, and that the mountains, half obscured in the evening light, were banks of dark clouds in the distance. We cannot say that the fireworks in any way enhanced the attraction of the fjord.

On our way back to the ship we caught up the three sisters and their brother, and we all stood for some minutes on the jetty, shouting to the *Venus* to send a boat for us. The six of us arranged to shout 'Boat, ahoy!' in unison, but someone would always commence to laugh just as the signal to start was given, and a great discord was the result. However, a boat came at last and took us on board, and we gave the sailor two kroner for working overtime, with which he seemed much delighted.

# CHAPTER XI

Letters from England—Island of Lepsö—Molde,
Its Church and Leprosy Hospital.

EARLY next morning, as we lay in our berths, we heard the rattle, rattle caused by the lowering of the anchor, and on looking out of our port-hole, we saw the ship was stopping at some place which we took to be Aalesund. But we were too comfortable to disturb ourselves, so we turned over, as the saying is, and went to sleep again. We wonder, by the way, whether anybody did ever wake up at night and go to sleep again without 'turning over,' at least in print.

By this time we were getting so accustomed to the various noises, that they ceased to have such a distracting effect as during the first few days of the cruise.

Even the 'early morning promenader's' malicious performance was losing some of its venom, but we were careful not to let him know it, or perhaps he would have devised some fresh method of disturbance. During the last few nights before we returned to Newcastle, we had grown so accustomed to sounds, that we believe, if the four guns had been fired at night, we should merely have muttered 'bother!' or some more or less innocent exclamation, should have performed the usual 'turn' and gone to sleep again.

The morning after the Lawyer returned to his bachelor quarters, he fancied he heard in the early hours the well-known tramp of his friend the promenader, and, of course, took no notice of it, but slumbered on peacefully for an hour or two. Afterwards he was surprised to learn that his domestic had been pummelling at his door for five minutes at a time, every half-hour, from half-past seven to ten o'clock, without the slightest effect. The gentle sound produced by the contact of knuckles with the door-panel was as nothing compared with the rasping clatter of the anchor-chain, or the tramp of the promenader.

At breakfast, the welcome news that the mail from England had come on board at Aalesund, and that there were letters in the office, passed round the tables like an electric current. Many eyes seemed to brighten, especially those of the engaged young man; most people hurried over the meal, and then there was a simultaneous rush to the office. It was only seven days since we left Newcastle, but everybody seemed anxious for news from home, and we had not seen an English newspaper for a whole week. On our second visit to Bergen, we inquired at Bennett's and found that the latest papers they had were those brought over by the *Venus*.

The Lawyer, unfortunately, found a telegram waiting for him, calling him back to England as soon as possible, but on consulting the Captain he was informed that it was very uncertain whether, if he left the *Venus* at Molde—the next stopping place—he could get back to England any sooner than by completing the cruise. So he decided to remain on board.

The Captain pointed out to us the Island of Lepsö, on which the fishing smack *Columbine* ran ashore in 1886, after having been blown from its moorings off the Shetland Islands, and drifting before the wind for eight days in the North Sea, with one woman, Mrs Mouat, on board, who was rescued by the islanders. We are almost ashamed to mention this story, as we believe it appears in every guide-book as a most interesting and important piece of history. If it had not been for this incident, the Island of Lepsö would be quite an unknown spot to ninety-nine out of every one hundred tourists.

A general topic of conversation during the morning, was an accident which befell the lady-of-noble-proportions at Merok. The account she gave of it was somewhat humorous. Accompanied by another lady, she drove in a stolkjarre up to Knuden, and either on the way up or coming down the pony fell flat on its side. Both ladies were thrown out, and she-of-noble-proportions suddenly found herself deposited on the top of the pony. And, as the lady narrated the story, 'the pony was so good, it never stirred for a minute or two until I was helped up, and what is more remarkable, that pony is *alive still.*' Most people thought the pony must have sustained a greater shock than the lady.

The *Venus* came to anchor off the pretty little town of Molde about eleven o'clock, and a number of prams and a steam launch were quickly alongside. Half-a-dozen of us were rowed ashore by a patriarchal old man with a long white beard, who could speak a little English, and assured us with great pride that he had been a waterman 'for forty *hours.*' We were so struck with this lengthy term that we inquired if we rightly understood him. 'Yes,' he replied, 'it's forty *hours* ago since I first rowed here.' The fine old man had evidently made a little mistake, but we did not like to correct him or ask how many minutes made up one of his hours. He could speak English much better than any of us Englishmen in his boat could speak Norwegian.

The Lawyer wanted to send a telegram to England, so we inquired for the post office and found it with very little trouble. However, when we reached it, we were told that telegrams were not despatched from the post office, and were directed to the telegraph office at the other end of the short main street. After finishing this business, we made our way to the church, in front of which a small crowd of 'Venuses' were assembled. It appeared that a service of some sort, either a wedding or a christening, we were told, was being held, and until it was over no one would be admitted.

The church is a modern wooden building of some pretensions, with a fine steeple, but its chief attraction is a large picture above the altar, painted by a Norwegian artist, depicting the visit of the two Marys to the tomb of our Saviour, and entitled 'Fear not, He is risen.' We were informed that the service would not be finished for an hour, so we turned into the main street again and walked towards the north end of the town, along a pretty road, lined on both sides with trees.

Molde has a delightful situation. In front are the placid lake-like blue waters of the fjord, several miles in width, and beyond, in a complete semi-circle, innumerable mountains, studded with white patches of snow, jut up into the sky. Behind the town, the ground rises in a gentle slope, thickly planted with trees, through which are many delightful walks. Some distance away is a small public park; but, as our stay was limited and the sun was very hot, we did not attempt to visit it.

Returning from the north end we went a short way up the hill and sat down under a mountain-ash tree, which was a perfect picture of pink and red colour. Here we waited in complete contentment for half-an-hour or so, until it was time for us to return to the steamer. We were very reluctant to go, as was often the case with us in Norway, but when hard-working parsons and lawyers and such like can only manage to get a fortnight's holiday, a long stay at any one place is impossible.

On our way back, we passed the church where the service was still proceeding, and in company with the three sisters we walked back to the quay. Here we were told that the Captain had decided to stop another hour so as to give us the opportunity of seeing the altar-piece. We accordingly sauntered back to the church and found that the congregation were just coming out. Three ladies dressed in white, accompanied by a few gentlemen, drove away in carriages, and perhaps thirty other people, in ordinary everyday garments, dispersed in different directions. Some ladies pronounced the ceremony to have been a christening, but as we did not see the indispensable baby, it appeared to us more like a wedding. It might, however, have been an adult christening. Be that as it may, it was finished, and a much larger congregation of 'Venuses' and others entered the church. The painting, to a non-professional mind, is certainly well-designed and effective, and the colours harmonise excellently. Many of our party were much impressed with it, and, probably, to some people it would serve as a great aid to devotion. The church is seated with English-looking benches, but there is nothing striking in the interior except the painting.

Our friend, the Doctor, had an introduction to the Norwegian doctor in charge of the Leprosy Hospital at Molde, and he, with others of our table, paid a visit to the Institution. It is situated at the south end of the town, close to the fjord, and is a fine-looking building. Our Doctor expressed himself as very pleased with all the arrangements of the hospital, which is kept in excellent order, and was highly interesting to him, from a professional point of view. The poor patients, however, presented a very piteous appearance, and drew forth the deep commiseration of the Doctor and his non-professional companions. It was a satisfaction to be informed that leprosy, which some attribute to the diet of dried fish, is rapidly decreasing in Norway; and, in consequence, the removal of the hospital from Molde is contemplated.

Our patriarchal, forty-hours'-experienced boatman rowed us back to the *Venus*, and charged us twenty-five orer a-piece for each journey—not an excessive charge.

# CHAPTER XII

### The Romsdal Fjord—Veblungsnæs and Aandalsnæs—Norwegian Ponies—The Romsdalhorn and Troldtinder—Hörgheim—The Mongefos.

SOON after leaving Molde, we went down to dinner, and when we came on deck again the *Venus* was sailing up the Romsdal Fjord, close to Naes. We are told that there are two villages of this name—Veblungsnæs and Aandalsnæs—one on each side of the river Rauma.

The end of the Romsdal Fjord is not quite so closely shut in by mountains as the Nærö or Geiranger Fjords, but still it is very grand, and behind Veblungsnæs stand some very fine snow-capped peaks. Several skydsguts who could speak English boarded the *Venus* at Molde, and we engaged one of them, provided his stolkjarre met with our approval, to drive us up the Romsdal Valley to Horgheim, and on to the Mongefos.

The three sisters and their brother were leaving the *Venus* at Naes, and as our stay only allowed just sufficient time for a drive to the Mongefos and back, we went on shore in the first boat, while the fair trio were busy in their cabins getting their luggage ready. As we neared the land, we saw them standing on the deck by the rail; and so they remain in our memory.

The landing-stage at Aandalsnæs was packed with dozens of skydsguts, so that it took some minutes to get through. The skydsgut we had engaged quickly found us, and took us to a stolkjarre with a very decent pony. As soon, however, as we had got in, he called a boy to drive us, and disappeared. We asked the boy if he could speak English, but he evidently did not understand what we said. We felt we had been somewhat done, and debated whether we should refuse to go with the boy. As, however, he was a nice-looking, tidy lad, and we wanted to get away before the other conveyances, we made signs to him to start. There were only two vehicles in front of us, and a long string of them were coming behind. Luckily, there was very little dust and no wind, so travelling in company did not much signify.

The Norwegian ponies go very well if they get a good lead, which is seldom the case, for the first pony, with the connivance of its skydsgut, considers it his duty, for the sake of his companions behind, to set a slow pace, averaging, when trotting, about six miles an hour, and he takes care always to walk not faster than two miles an hour up every hill, including the most gentle rise.

One peculiarity we noticed in driving in Norway, besides keeping to the right-hand side of the road when meeting another vehicle, was that every few miles along the road is placed a water trough, and at each of these the skydsgut pulls up and allows the pony to drink its fill of the water, which is often icy cold, having just fallen from the snowfield at the top of an adjoining mountain.

In England this would be considered likely to end in the premature death of the pony, but these Norwegian-bred animals seem to thrive. The ponies are sturdy little creatures, averaging about thirteen hands, and are generally in good condition. The skydsguts treat them kindly, and are careful not to over-drive them. We always endeavoured to pick out a strong pony in good condition, and as the majority of tourists do the same, it does not pay to harness a poor animal. Of course, at the inland posting-stations, where the traveller has to change ponies, he is bound to take what is given him. At the villages at the end of the fjords, however, we always found more vehicles waiting than were wanted, so that it was possible to choose between them.

Most of the country roads in Norway are only just wide enough to allow of two carioles passing, and one has to pull up at the very edge of the road while the other creeps slowly by. If, as is often the case, there is a drop, varying from six to one hundred feet, on one side of the road, the meeting of two carioles or stolkjarrer causes some excitement.

At a turn in the road, soon after leaving Aandalsnaes, the Romsdalhorn came into full view, towering up in front of us, and appearing to block the valley completely. Its curious sugar-loaf shaped cone, pointing to the sky, was free from snow, patches of which were clinging to the mountain in many places lower down. The view of the Romsdalhorn across the Rauma, here widening out into a small lake, is very fine. The mountains, before the Romsdalhorn is reached, stand back a little way from the river, and the intervening space in many parts is thickly wooded, and elsewhere divided into lawn-like meadows, beautifully green in colour. On the other side of the river rises the Troldtinder mountain, with several jagged peaks higher than the Romsdalhorn by nearly one hundred feet; but the Troldtinder does not stand out so conspicuously as the mountain that gives its name to, or derives it from, the fjord.

In this drive, and also on many previous occasions, we saw several magpies, often seven or eight together. These, and the greyish-black rooks, were the birds most frequently met with, for we did not notice very many small birds.

The road runs round the foot of the mighty —we feel bound to follow the guide books in using this adjective—Romsdalhorn, and here the valley becomes much narrower, widening out again after the mountain is passed. Horgheim figures so prominently in the guide books that we expected to see at least a fair-sized village. We noticed that the stolkjarre in front of us pulled up at a small wayside posting-station, resembling a country public house in England, with one cottage close by to keep it from feeling lonely, but not another habitation in sight. We wondered what we were stopping here for, and as our skydsgut could not understand us, we asked one of those in front. He replied that it was Horgheim, and that a stop of twenty minutes was always made here to rest the ponies. We fancy this must have been an arrangement between the keeper of the inn and the skydsguts for their mutual benefit. Nearly all the 'fares' went into the station, and, no doubt, consumed numerous drinks of various descriptions. We virtuously determined not to be bamboozled into drinking, at least, not this time, and, after waiting a few minutes, we made our boy understand that we should walk on, and that he could come after us when his pony was sufficiently rested. We thought, indeed, that the pony had been resting most of the way from Naes.

Our example was followed by the two Frenchmen, fellow 'Venuses,' and the four of us walked on for a mile or so before our companions' conveyance caught us up, and they drove on. Our boy came up soon after, and his pony, seeing the other some way ahead, trotted along bravely, and it was not long before we came in sight of the fall. When close to it, we passed, on the right-hand side of the road, a farm-house with several reindeer antlers lying on the ground in front. These excited the wrath of an Indian sportsman, one of the 'Venuses,' as will be presently seen.

The road runs straight past the Mongefos,

about five hundred yards from it, and the Frenchmen and we decided to attempt to get nearer. We saw a grass-covered road leading in the right direction, so we opened the gate and walked on. This presently led us to a most romantic, garden-like wood of pine trees, growing between boulders of rock, some of immense size, scattered about in charming confusion, and in places almost touching one another. We followed a footpath winding in and out amongst, and sometimes over, these boulders, while frequently we could not see more than a few yards ahead. It was really a most remarkable wood, and possessed an unique fascination; but not one, out of many dozen tourists, except ourselves left the road. Presently we came to the river some distance from the foot of the fall, which here took the form of a very pretty rapid.

The Mongejura, over which the Mongefos pours itself, is 4230 feet high, so that the fall is a very considerable one; as regards the quantity of water, however, it is not to be compared with the Laatefos.

We suddenly caught sight of some animals moving amongst the trees and rocks, but could not at first make them out as they were so obscured by the leaves. We went towards them, hoping that they might be reindeer, and found they were only goats. The reindeer would be high up on the mountains in the summer, as we might have reflected, but at the moment did not.

We returned to our conveyance, much pleased with our walk, and started back to Naes. On passing the farm we found the shikaree who had been to inspect the antlers, and he remarked to us, in indignant tones,—'Have you seen those antlers? Why, the deer have all been shot while in the velvet, a most unjustifiable and barbarous proceeding, which, if not forbidden by the Norwegian law, ought to be!'

On the way back we greatly amused our skydsgut and ourselves by carrying on, or rather attempting to carry on, a conversation with him by means of the glossary appended to 'Baedeker.' The boy, judging from his repeated hearty laughter, considered it a highly comic entertainment. Then we pointed out a hawk, hovering over the trees growing high up on the side of one of the mountains. He insisted it was a crow, but we were equally certain it was a hawk. We found the word 'hawk' in 'Baedeker' and drew his attention to the Norwegian equivalent. He read it, looked intently at the bird, which had come a little nearer, and then broke into a loud laugh, and exclaimed,— 'Falcon! ya! ya!'

On the left-hand side of the road, not far from Naes, we noticed a very picturesque garden, laid out in English fashion, and gay with geraniums and other flowers. The hedges were trimmed, and everything was nicely arranged and in neat order. We could not see much of the house, as it was partly hidden by trees and shrubs. We inquired of the boy by signs to whom the house belonged, and he replied,— 'Englishman, Worrouch,' or a word that sounded something like that. We did not recognise any familiar English name, and speculated as to what it could be. Afterwards we learnt that the place belonged to Mr Wills, of Bristol, well-known to smokers, and 'Worrouch' was the nearest approach to Wills that our skydsgut could manage.

It was past nine o'clock before we were again on board, but as nearly all the passengers had driven to the Mongefos, supper was not served until half-past nine. A German gentleman, who joined the *Venus* at Bergen and sat at our table, had been fishing in the fjord from the vessel, and to his surprise, he had caught, besides several whiting, a cod over a yard long, which was an unexpected prize, and gave considerable trouble before it was hauled on deck.

# CHAPTER XIII

The Hustadvik Headland—Christianssund—Trondhjem—Absence of Slums—Broken-down Bridge—The Lower and Upper Lerfos.

THE *Venus* left Naes while we were at supper, and was timed to reach Molde in about two hours, merely stopping there long enough to embark a few passengers, and then proceeding to Christianssund the next point of call. We had, during the night or early morning, to pass round the Hustadvik headland, where there is no chain of islands to break the Atlantic swell, and as it was blowing rather hard we fully expected to be tossed about. We retired to our berths before arriving at Molde, and slept so soundly that the lowering and raising of the anchor did not disturb us. In the early morning we were conscious that the boat was rolling and pitching somewhat, and this continued until after breakfast. Many on board were rather relieved when we got into calmer water close to Christianssund.

The approach to this port from the south is rather curious, as the town is quite hidden from view until the vessel enters the narrow inlet between the islands. The *Venus* slowed down, and we were told that Christianssund was just ahead, but to our astonishment we could see nothing whatever of the town. The ship was steaming slowly towards a rocky island a short distance away, and we could perceive no opening, and no buildings were visible. We almost expected the island to be drawn up like the curtain at a theatre and disclose the town just behind. Presently we came close to the island and a little opening appeared, which gradually widened as we approached it obliquely. Entering this we found ourselves in an almost circular harbour, around which the town of Christianssund is built.

The red-tiled warehouses and buildings are picturesquely packed together close to the water, and the harbour was alive with fishing boats, rowing boats, large and small, and two or three steamers.

As soon as the anchor was down, we went on shore, walked along the main street and shortly found ourselves at a large church, close to which was a pretty park thickly planted with trees. We could not enter the church as it was locked, so we strolled down two or three more streets and then made our way back to the wharf.

The harbour and the open space at the quay seemed the most attractive part of Christianssund. On the other side of the harbour, near the inlet at which we entered, were numerous little round stacks, like miniature haystacks, of dried fish, with peculiar white umbrella-shaped covers on the top of them. The whole place has rather a fishy smell, but we did not find it so pronounced as in the old Hanseatic quarter at Bergen.

The *Venus* was only to remain at Christianssund two hours, so we were soon on board again. We did not, however, start at the appointed time, as the Captain was still on shore. The numerous telescopes and field-glasses on board were directed towards the quay to ascertain the whereabouts of our missing chief, and presently he was seen in front of one of the warehouses talking to another man, no doubt on the Bergenske Dampskibsselskab business. Shortly after, he left the quay in a little boat, and his heavy weight sent the gunwale down almost level with the water.

We left Christianssund through an opening between the islands opposite to where we entered, and all the afternoon we sailed north-east up the coast, past the Smolen and Hitteren Islands and dozens of small islets, the names of which we know not.

The *Venus* entered the Trondhjem Fjord about eight o'clock in the evening while we were at supper, and when we returned on deck we were approaching the city. The vessel was moored to the quay about an hour later, and as soon as the gangway was down we went on shore.

Trondhjem, when viewed from the water, has a much more pretentious appearance than Bergen. The quays have quite a noble width and will accommodate a large number of vessels. The warehouses, too, are larger than those at Bergen, and altogether Trondhjem is not unlike Southampton on a smaller scale.

After following the road for half a mile and crossing the railway, we found ourselves in a broad street with handsome wooden houses on each side. We wanted to make our way to the Cathedral, as we concluded it would be somewhere in the centre of the town, and we inquired the way of a man who could not understand English, but he very courteously stopped another man who was able to speak our language, and the latter put us in the right direction.

Trondhjem contains, we are told, about 26,000 inhabitants, and is the most northerly of the larger towns of Europe, the latitude being the same as that of the south coast of Iceland. What struck us particularly at Trondhjem and also at Bergen was the entire absence of any 'slums.' We walked through both towns in various directions, yet we never once came across any slummy quarter. The streets, especially in Trondhjem, were invariably wide and the houses nicely painted and in good repair. We did not see any dirty, squalid cottage dwellings, such as are always in evidence in the back streets of an English town of any size. Perhaps they exist; but, if so, they must be very cleverly hidden away: if there are none, the Norwegians must manage matters very much better than we do.

We did not succeed in finding the Cathedral that night. We walked up and down several streets, looking into the shop windows, and taking note of anything that interested us. We came to a large church standing at the end of a street of even greater width than usual, and we took this to be the Cathedral, but were disappointed with the architecture, which was not imposing. When we returned to the ship, we compared notes with some of our friends, and were glad to find that the building we had taken for the Cathedral was merely a church, and that the Cathedral was a much more imposing structure.

We slept on board, having acquired quite a liking for our comfortable little cabin, and it seemed scarcely worth while going to an hotel for the one night.

The next morning the sun was shining gloriously, and the Scotchman and we considered the exercise of a long tramp would do us good, so we set off after breakfast to walk to the Lerfos, which, according to 'Baedeker,' is about five kilometres from Trondhjem, or four hours' walk there and back. We passed through the town and again admired the wide streets and picturesque wooden houses. We noticed that a large piece of zinc roofing had become loosened by the wind and was hanging in a very dangerous position over the doorway of a jeweller's shop. The Scotchman went in and informed the shopwoman, who spoke excellent English; she came out to look at the threatening danger, and then thanked us very politely. On our return, the workmen were on the roof repairing the damage.

Just as we left Trondhjem we passed a

rather fine church, but we did not attempt to see the interior. It possesses· a clock with a very peculiar face, apparently designed with the intention of preventing anyone from ascertaining the time. At Ihlen is a pretty garden-like park, very thickly planted with trees and shrubs, but we did not enter it as our road turned off to the left. A mile from Trondhjem we had a fine view of the city, encircled by the winding river Nid, the Cathedral and Arsenal being very conspicuous. Presently our road ran by the side of the river, and here we came upon an object that excited our curiosity but we could find no reference to it in 'Baedeker.' From the other side of the Nid, which is here 150 yards or so in width, the arches of a strong, stone-built bridge stretch across the water, but two arches on our side were missing. We wondered whether the builders had commenced their work without correctly estimating the cost and had to stop for want of funds, or if the bridge had been broken down in war, or by a flood, and never repaired. Whatever may be its history, the old broken-down bridge has a very forlorn and suggestive appearance, and as we stood looking at it our thoughts turned to the traditional New Zealander who is one day to stand on the ruins of London Bridge.

Soon after passing the bridge, the road leaves the river, and on the left hand is a good-sized corn mill. We inquired here how far it was to the Lerfos, and were given to understand that we had still a long way to go, as it proved. At length, after a steep hill, we came to a thick wood of pine trees, and we were delighted to hear in the distance the faint thunder of the fall. At the entrance to the wood we met a Norwegian peasant girl, who, as she passed us, smiled and pointed to a 'Baedeker' she carried in her hand, as if to ask whether it belonged to us. We shook our heads, and the Lawyer pointed to his copy in his pocket. The girl seemed to understand us and walked on, laughing as she went. If she intended to trudge all the way to Trondhjem, and there to seek for the owner of the book, she would well earn any reward she was likely to get. If a reward was not her primary object, and she was endeavouring to restore the book to its owner for the sake of honesty, taking, moreover, so much trouble about it, the integrity of the Norwegian folk must be of a high type.

For about a quarter of an hour we proceeded through the wood and then reached an inn of considerable size, standing close beside, but on higher ground than, the fall. The declivity down which the Lower Lerfos descends is not very great, being about eighty feet, and is far from the perpendicular, but a large volume of water pours over, between and around some rocks at the top, and the sight is certainly a grand one—not, however, equal to the Laatefos. For many people, there is a wonderful fascination in watching a mass of water rushing and thundering down a precipice, and we are not free from that weakness.

The Upper Lerfos is higher up the river, a good quarter-of-an-hour's walk from the lower. The path leading to it is very pretty, running along by the side of the river, with several twists and turns through pine-tree woods. We came upon a squirrel feeding on the ground here, within six yards of us, and he did not betray the slightest fear, but continued playing about while we stood watching him. His behaviour was very different to that of his timid brothers and sisters in England.

We were a little disappointed with the Upper Lerfos, although it has a certain picturesqueness of its own. We did not go close to it, but we were told that the best view is obtained from an old saw-mill on the right bank, projecting over the water.

We did not at all enjoy our walk back to Trondhjem, as the road was very dusty and the sun scorching. We afterwards learnt that we might have come back by train, which we would gladly have done.

It was a source of wonder to us that the heat could be so great and affect us so much in such a high latitude. Very glad we were to reach the Britannia Hotel, where we enjoyed a good dinner.

# CHAPTER XIV

Trondhjem Cathedral and Arsenal — Shops at Trondhjem — Homeward Bound — Christiansund—Molde—Aalesund—A Scramble.

IN the afternoon we determined to visit the Cathedral, or Domkirke as it is called in the guide books; and on reaching it we found we had some time to wait before we could be admitted, so we strolled round the burial-ground and looked at the quaint Norwegian graves, many of which are encircled by a fence and have a seat whereon the relatives of the departed may rest and meditate.

Returning to the door, we were joined by some 'typical tourists,' a man and two ladies, not 'Venuses,' who were also waiting to 'do' the Cathedral. At six o'clock the door was opened by an attendant who spoke

English fluently, and we entered the building through the chapter-house. Our guide told us that the Government granted an annual subsidy of we forget how many thousand pounds towards the building fund, which made the Parson's mouth water as he thought of a little church at home sadly needing restoration. While engaged in these reflections, he was nearly knocked down by 'the typical tourists,' who were hastily leaving the sacred edifice, having 'done' it in about five minutes.

Originally a basilica, built over the burial-place of King Olaf the Saint, enlarged in the middle of the 12th century to receive the thousands of pilgrims visiting the sacred shrine, re-enlarged in the 13th century, partially burnt in the 14th, 15th, 16th, and twice in the 17th centuries, this mother-church of Norway is a mixture of Romanesque, Gothic and Ornate-Gothic styles of architecture, and is well worthy of careful inspection. The rich mouldings of the triforium windows in the east end are most elaborate, and all different, but some of them were left unfinished seven hundred years ago, and remain so now.

The east end only has been restored, and this is temporarily separated from the west end, now in the hands of the workmen. When the whole of the building is finished and opened, the portion at present used for service might, not incorrectly, be described as the choir and chancel, and the west end as the nave. At the extreme east end of the restored building is an octagonal apse-like chancel, and on an altar in the centre of it, the relics of Saint Olaf were placed prior to the Reformation. The attendant told us that the massive silver reliquary containing the relics was taken to Copenhagen at the time of the Reformation, but the outer wooden chest still remains and was shown to us.

In a recess on the south side of the apse is Saint Olaf's Well, supposed to have sprung up, as the guide told us, on the spot where the saint was originally buried. We inquired whether there was still any water in the well, but the guide did not appear to know. The well is about four feet in diameter, and is surrounded by a low stone parapet. We looked down, but, of course, could not see the bottom, and had no means of trying its depth.

The Cathedral is interesting on historical grounds, but we do not propose to refer to that subject further than to mention that the Kings of Norway and Sweden are crowned first at Stockholm and then in the Cathedral at Trondhjem.

The west end is still in a most unfinished state, but the Norwegians show their good sense by trying to rebuild all parts exactly as they were in bygone times, and, when finished, Trondhjem Cathedral will be well worthy of a high place amongst the historic buildings of Europe.

After leaving the Cathedral, we decided to visit the Arsenal close at hand. The guide book told us that admission to it could be obtained on application to the sentry, but the book did not follow the praiseworthy example of the old cookery book, and tell us that it was necessary in the first place to catch the sentry. We walked into and about the courtyard, and searched diligently for that sentry, but could not see any trace of him. If there was such a gentlemen on guard, he concealed himself very effectually somewhere. Possibly he thought we looked dangerous, and, like the traditional policeman at the prospect of a row, had a pressing engagement elsewhere.

However, we saw all that was to be seen from the courtyard, which 'all' consisted principally of the under and some of the outer clothing of the garrison, hung out on the balcony to dry. Not wishing to intrude into such-like domestic matters, we beat a leisurely retreat and invaded two or three shops instead, where we had no difficulty in finding someone on the lookout.

We had heard that very fair cigars could be bought at Trondhjem for not much more than half their price in England, the duty on tobacco in Norway being very light. So we purchased a hundred cigars and the same number of cigarettes. We should have bought many more had not we been doubtful as to the quantity we could bring, not smuggle, into England free of duty.

It appears to us that the shops at Trondhjem are quite equal, if not superior, to those at Bergen. Nearly every visitor to Norway spends a day or two at Bergen, but a great many do not go so far north as Trondhjem, and consequently the shops at the latter place do not seem to be quite so ransacked by the tourist as those at Bergen.

The *Venus* sailed from Trondhjem at midnight; we stayed on deck until she got under weigh on the homeward voyage, and then retired to our berths, regretting that we were no longer outward bound. We had not found the cruise at all monotonous, and would gladly have gone on to the North Cape if the chains of duty and business had not dragged us back to England.

The following morning we arrived at Christianssund, where we made only a short stay. We did not go on shore this visit, the movement in the harbour amongst the fishing boats, flats and prams being quite sufficient to interest us. Some of the passengers landed, and one lady was nearly left behind. The anchor was up, the whistle had sounded more than once, and we wondered why we did not start. The second mate then hurried round the ship, looking for some one, and explained that he was searching for a lady who had gone ashore and, he had been told, had not returned. His search was unsuccessful, the whistle was blown again, and shortly after we saw a boat put off from the other side of the harbour, in the stern of which sat the missing lady, energetically waving her parasol to attract the Captain's attention. As the boat drew near, we saw that it was manned by an elderly man and two young women, probably his daughters, and the four oars—the man rowed with a pair—kept beautiful time as the crew pulled their hardest to catch the ship, which was just on the move.

The women rowed wonderfully well, and their light pram travelled through the water at a very good rate. How would these two strong young Norwegian fisherwomen shape as a pair at Henley?

The lady was profuse in her apologies to the Captain for delaying the ship, and explained that her dilatoriness arose from a mistake as regards the time. The principal towns in Norway appear to regulate their clocks according to the geographical situation of the locality, so that during our cruise we found it necessary to compare our watches with the ship's time nearly every morning. The Captain assured the lady that as he had the mails on board, he could not have waited any longer for her, and that if she had been left behind he should have placed her luggage in the Company's office at Bergen. It would have been very unfortunate for the lady to have been separated from her luggage without any possibility of getting it for two or three days.

It was very pleasant sailing back down

the coast, and we enjoyed it quite as much as the voyage up. The ever-changing panorama of mountains, islands and rocks, sunlit sea and blue sky presented many delightful pictures that varied too frequently to become monotonous. We cannot imagine a more delicious way of spending a summer's afternoon, than sailing along the coast of Norway, in smooth water, comfortably seated on a deck chair, with the companionship of a favourite book, or, better still, a like-minded companion of the opposite sex. The cool sea breeze tempers the heat of the sun, and the book or the companion absorbs all such stray faculties as may not be occupied with the scenery; or, perhaps, that is neglected and almost forgotten in the presence of softer and more winning charms. Nothing more delightful, did we say? Ah, well, we think we must make one exception to this summit of summer afternoon happiness, and that is, an even match at golf over a good green, with a clear course, and *no* companion of the opposite sex.

The *Venus* touched at Molde about four o'clock, and we went on shore again for a walk along the pretty tree-planted road. We did not on this occasion see the ancient forty-hours'-experienced boatman but patronised the steam launch.

We reached Aalesund in the evening, and the ship was moored to the quay. We were to stop here about two hours, so we went on shore and walked through the little town to the small public park situate .on high ground at the back, from which a very picturesque view of the town and fjord is obtained. Aalesund has the quaint old-world look associated in one's mind with mediæval cities, no doubt attributable to the wooden houses and the irregularity of the streets, and perhaps also to the curious build of the Norwegian prams floating in the harbour and fjord.

The *Venus* did not start for some little time after we were on board, and we amused ourselves with watching a small crowd of children playing about on the wharf close by. They evidently wished to attract the attention of the 'Venuses,' and in this were completely successful. A lady on board happened to have with her a small [bag of gooseberries, and she gave them to the Parson to scramble amongst the children. The Parson scattered them with professional skill, as if he had been at a school treat in England, but to the chagrin and astonishment of us all, not a single child picked one up, or betrayed the slightest concern or curiosity. They regarded the whole proceeding as utterly beneath them and unworthy of notice. After some few minutes, one little boy, in a half-apologetic manner, did pick up one gooseberry and eat it. Then his companions, observing that it had no immediate ill effect on him and that he was going for another, seemed to consider that they might as well waive their dignity, and all the gooseberries disappeared a moment later. Judging from this incident, it might be conjectured that scrambling is not one of the excitements indulged in at school treats in Norway.

Just before we sailed, a Wilson boat put off from an adjoining quay. She flew a large flag announcing that she was chartered by some religious association, the name of which we forget, and she appeared to be crowded with people. One of the Irishmen at once pronounced her to be a teetotal boat, and expressed his profound sympathy for her unfortunate passengers who had to cross the North Sea twice without an alleviating whisky-and-soda.

The *Venus* called at Moldoen and Floro during the night, and the following morning, soon after breakfast, we steamed up the beautiful approach to Bergen, and the ship was soon moored to the quay, in the familiar position near the Kongshall. We were glad to spend another day in Bergen, as there were many objects of interest which we had not been able to see on our first visit.

# CHAPTER XV

Bergen Museum—Old Wooden Church at Fantoft—Ironing the North Sea, and the Result—The Tyne and the Custom-House Officers.

MINDFUL of our former experience at Bergen, we carefully avoided the Tydskebryggen with its fishy aroma, and walked through the town to the Bergen Museum. This is located in a large, handsome building, in what an English auctioneer would describe as 'the best residential part' of the town, a mile or so from where the *Venus* was moored. We were agreeably surprised at the variety and extent of the collection, no less than the excellent method of arrangement. Of course it can scarcely be compared with the British Museum or South Kensington, but we doubt whether, out of London, its equal can be found in England. We should certainly advise anyone who appreciates museums not to omit to visit this one when in Bergen.

In the afternoon we intended to drive to Fantoft, but, as the Parson was indisposed, we relinquished the idea. However, we had a description of the old wooden church from some of our friends who visited it, and described it as very quaint, unique and most interesting. It originally stood at Fortun on the Sogne Fjord, and was removed to its present position in the grounds of the American Consul.

The *Venus* was to sail for Newcastle at nine o'clock, and many of the passengers who had rather an unpleasant experience on the voyage out, were looking forward with no little dread to the vagaries of the North Sea. Most of us, at any rate, determined to make a good supper, not knowing whether we should feel equal to eating much during the next thirty-six hours. It is very nice, when comfortably seated in a drawing-room that has not the pernicious habit of turning one side wall uppermost and then another, to hear a pretty young lady sweetly sing about the pleasures of being 'rocked in the cradle of the deep' and boasting about her 'peaceful sleep' in that luxurious couch. But the same young lady and the applauders of her song, when rocked somewhat vigorously in the actual cradle, generally sing, if capable of doing so at all, a strain of a different complexion, interspersed with frequent exclamations of 'Oh dear! Oh dear!'

The Captain came into the smoking saloon after supper, just before starting, and said, 'Tell the ladies I've had the North Sea ironed down, so they need not be afraid.' This announcement was at least intended to be comforting, and was duly communicated by the smokers to their lady relations and friends, but it was told and received with a certain amount of hesitation, akin to that with which the patient hears the dentist's assurance that the extracting of a tooth 'won't hurt.'

Nearly all the passengers were on deck when the Captain stationed himself on the bridge, and gave the order to unmoor from the wharf. As we left the harbour, many regretful glances were turned towards Bergen and its surrounding mountains and hills, which were all too soon shut out of view, owing to a bend in the fjord. We are sure that a number of people consoled themselves with the reflection that next year they would again visit the country, and further explore its many beauties.

We remained on deck until the pilot was put off the ship into a small boat, just before we reached the open sea. Then the Parson retired, with the intention of getting comfortably to sleep in smooth water; the Lawyer, however, stopped on deck to see the last of Norway.

As soon as the *Venus* was fairly outside the last island, she encountered some heavy rollers, which evidently were not expected by the stewards. When the first one struck the ship, she suddenly commenced to roll very prettily, and in an instant all the glasses and water-bottles in the smoking saloon, except one the Lawyer managed to hold on to, slid off the tables, and according to their nature, distributed themselves in many pieces about the floor. The next moment there was a great crash in the saloon below, and several of us, on looking down to see what had happened, found that various dishes of cold meat, ham and tongue, which had been lying on the outer saloon table, had followed the example of the glasses and bottles in the smoking saloon, and were resting on the floor. It was quite clear that the Captain's 'ironing' had not been so entirely effectual as he had led us to believe, but the stewards seem to have placed some faith in it.

Not long after this, the Lawyer thought his berth would be the most comfortable spot on board, and went below. He found some difficulty in disrobing, owing to being shot from side to side in the small box-like space, meanwhile the Parson was jeering at him in a most unparsonical manner. That difficulty, however, was not insurmountable, and we were soon both snugly ensconced, not sleeping, but listening to the noise of the wind and sea beating against the ship, and a terrific crashing in the forehold, caused, as we fancied, by crates of empty bottles, not properly secured, sliding about at every roll of the ship, and being brought up suddenly by contact with one another or the side of the hold. When this had been going on for some little time, the sailors must have made them fast, for the noise stopped, and we drifted unconsciously into dreamland.

The next morning, Sunday, the sea had gone down a little, for the ship was not moving about in quite so lively a fashion as during the previous evening, but there was still a good deal of motion on. After comparing notes, we congratulated ourselves that neither of us felt any the worse for the tossing, and we were quite ready to do full justice to the breakfast. The cooks must have had rather a light task that morning in preparing the repast, as scarcely a dozen men were in the saloon with us, and, alas! not a single lady. Of course, some may have breakfasted later. The fiddles were fixed to the tables, and prevented the plates and dishes from wandering on to the floor.

A service was held in the saloon during the morning, but only ten persons were present, the large majority of passengers being either totally incapacitated from enjoying anything, or in a somewhat dubious state. The latter, the Lawyer amongst them, considered the fresh air of the deck more congenial to their condition of body and mind than the saloon.

The sea became rather quieter as the day passed, and considerately allowed about half the passengers to sit down to dinner and supper. Nothing of any moment occurred during the day, and as there was no inducement to keeping late hours, we, like most of the 'Venuses,' retired early.

When we awoke the next morning, we found we were in the Tyne, slowly steaming up to the Albert Edward Dock. After breakfast, the luggage of all the passengers was overhauled by the custom-house officers, and some amusing incidents occurred. One gentleman declared three little silver spoons, value about fifteen shillings, and was very wroth at having to fill up and sign a long declaration. When the Lawyer produced a box originally containing fifty cigars, several of which had already been converted into smoke, the officer at once pronounced the box to contain one hundred. Unfortunately it did not. One of the Irishmen, when threatened with a claim for duty on some cigars, remarked that he preferred to throw them overboard, and met with the reply that he must not throw his own cigars into the dock until Her Majesty's duty thereon had been paid. On the whole, however, the officers performed their unpleasant duty in a very creditable manner.

A special train conveyed all the passengers and their luggage to the Newcastle Central Station, where we dispersed—as the ancient writer poetically expresses it—to the four winds of heaven.

We hope no one will be deterred from visiting Norway owing to dread of a very unpleasant experience while crossing the North Sea. The passage to Bergen only occupies thirty-six hours, to Stavanger rather less, and if the sea should unfortunately prove unkind, the time is soon over. After a day in Norway the spirits and appetite recover in a marvellous manner; and the delightful air and scenery amply compensate for the temporary inconvenience, which, after it is over, is generally treated as a subject for jest. The little annoyances and drawbacks, necessarily associated with a sea voyage, are more to be laughed over than grumbled at, and they resemble the shadows that serve to throw the beauties of a picture into greater prominence. We can imagine no better holiday for a hard-worked professional or business man, requiring rest, freedom from letters and business worries, and change of scenery, than a Yachting Cruise to Norway.

---

COLSTON AND COMPANY, LTD., PRINTERS, EDINBURGH.

www.ingramcontent.com/pod-product-compliance
Lightning Source LLC
Chambersburg PA
CBHW031446160426
43195CB00010BB/867